C000241253

Praise for Jul

'This is page-turningly unputdownable … I started off
thinking I would read the first chapter but stood up
many hours later, cold, stiff and hungry –
I had read the whole thing!
A great holiday read, or in my case an "at home"
distraction.'
Andrea McLean — *Loose Women TV Presenter*

'I wrongly assumed it would be lightweight, formulaic
chick-lit that would be an enjoyable read but little else.
I was wrong. It is well written with a pace that grips the
reader and there are believable characters that I wanted
to know more about.
The plot is exciting and entertaining. I loved the twists
and turns and the dramatic events that took place.'
Linda's Book Bag

'**Entertaining & Heart-Felt Emotions** – Julia Roberts
writes believable story-lines for characters that come
across as real and imperfect. Holly's story is captivating
and emotional and leaves me looking forward to
reading the final book of the trilogy.'
David Reviews — *Top 500 Reviewer on Amazon.co.uk*

Julia Roberts' passion for writing began when, at the age of ten, after winning second prize in a short story-writing competition, she announced that she wanted to write a book. After a small gap of forty-seven years, and a career in the entertainment industry, Julia finally fulfilled her dream in 2013 when her first book, a memoir entitled *One Hundred Lengths of the Pool*, was published by Preface Publishing. Two weeks later she had the idea for her first novel, *Life's a Beach and Then…*, book one in the Liberty Sands Trilogy, which was released in May 2015. Julia still works full-time as a Presenter for the TV channel QVC, where she has just celebrated her twenty-second anniversary.

She now lives in Ascot with her 'other half' of thirty-eight years and occasionally one or other of her children and their respective cats.

You can find out more about Julia and her books on her Facebook page www.facebook.com/JuliaRobertsTV and her website www.juliarobertsbooks.co.uk

You can also follow her on Twitter @JuliaRobertsQVC

By Julia Roberts
One Hundred Lengths of the Pool
Liberty Sands Trilogy:
Life's a Beach and Then…
If He Really Loved Me…
It's Never Too Late To Say…

It's Never
Too Late To Say...

Julia Roberts

A *ripped* book

Book three in the

Liberty Sands Trilogy

CHAPTER 1

Carol shivered beneath the pile of blankets on her bed. They were heavy but provided little warmth as they pressed her slight body into the sagging mattress. January and February had been mild and damp in the UK and had lulled everyone into thinking that spring was in the air, but in late March an arctic wind had swept across the country depositing heavy snow. The single-glazed, ill-fitting bedroom windows rattled and did little to keep the cold at bay and the flimsy curtains occasionally flapped in the draught, allowing light from the street-lamp to spill into the room and create strange-shaped shadows in the corners.

Carol felt her heart beating loudly against her ribcage. Someone was in the room with her; she could sense it. Easing herself up, she drew her knees into her chest to make herself as small as possible and pulled the covers up to her chin. She peered fearfully into the dark, unaware of the whimpering noise she was making, like a neglected dog. The wind gusted again, causing the curtains to billow inwards and, in the flash of illumination, a figure standing next to her bedroom door became clearly visible. She gasped.

'It's all right, Carol. No one's going to hurt you.'

The figure began to advance towards her.

'Mummy! Mummy!' she tried to cry out, but no sound came.

Two strong hands pushed her back on to her pillows. 'Shh, shh. It'll be over soon.'

Carol closed her eyes to block out the face but it was no good, it was imprinted on her mind. She could feel hot breath on her cheeks. 'Please, not again,' she begged in an almost inaudible whisper. 'I don't want to.' She opened her eyes to see a hand being lowered towards her face. It was a risk, but she had to take it. She grabbed the hand and bit down on it hard.

'Shit! What did you do that for?'

Carol squirmed out of the bed and, gathering all her strength, hurried towards the door. Footsteps closed in on her as she stumbled across the dark landing. If I can just reach Mummy's room and prove to her that I wasn't telling lies, Carol thought, then maybe she will love me again. A hand gripped her shoulder but, with an almighty effort, she pulled away, tripping on the hem of her nightgown. Terrified, she staggered forward, reaching out for the handrail of the staircase but her hands were so cold she couldn't grip and she plummeted headfirst down the stairs, landing at the bottom with a sickening thud.

'Carol, Carol, are you all right?' a woman's voice asked.

That doesn't sound like Mummy, Carol thought.

The last thing she heard before slipping into unconsciousness was the woman's voice saying, 'Ambulance, please. There's been an accident.'

CHAPTER 2

Holly felt like a caged tiger as she anxiously paced the small square room, clenching and unclenching her fists in an effort to calm herself. She had received the call at around 8.30 a.m. Fortunately, her son Harry was home from university for the Easter holidays so she was able to leave her baby daughter Rosie with him otherwise she couldn't have come. What am I even doing here? she thought, examining the pale face and unruly dark curls reflected back at her from a large mirror above a counter top, which was empty apart from a box of tissues. Is this really what I want? I could be at home right now puréeing carrots for Rosie's lunch instead of putting myself through this. There was a tap on the door.

'Come in,' Holly said tentatively. 'Oh, Philippe, thank goodness it's you. Perhaps you'd like to explain what's going on? Madison didn't say much on the phone. She just told me to get here as soon as possible, which wasn't easy with all this snow.'

'I'm sorry, Holly,' Philippe said, pulling her into a hug. 'I would have called you myself but I barely had time to mention you and give Maddie your details before I was needed in the studio. I'm glad you could come. I think you're just what they're looking for. Where's Rosie? I was hoping for a little daddy-and-daughter time while you're doing your audition.'

'I left her at home with Harry. I didn't know if you would still be here or whether you would have rushed off to your next TV appearance. Besides, I didn't think it would look very professional if I turned up with a baby in tow.'

'You've got a point there but it's nearly a month since I've had a cuddle with my princess. This tour itinerary is crazy. No one seems to know their geography at Ripped Publishing. They've got me in Scotland one minute and Cornwall the next, sometimes on the same day. It's madness! I'm not sure when they think I've got time to write the next book. Did I tell you they want to release it this autumn? There's no chance of that, I haven't even come up with a plot yet.'

Holly held her hands up in a 'don't look at me for inspiration' gesture, which seemed to take the edge off his irritation. She had finally forgiven him for using their passionate affair as the basis for *Tiffany*, his second book, but after three months their fledgling relationship was still limited to the occasional dinner out or quiet night in. It was clear to Holly that Philippe would have liked to regain the intimacy they had shared in Mauritius but although her kisses were eager and responsive she wasn't ready to trust him again yet, particularly with all the female attention he was getting since the book's release. Philippe would have to be patient, not a characteristic he was naturally blessed with.

'Philippe, I need you to fill me in on what I'm supposed

to be doing before they call for me. I'm really nervous. I've never done anything like this before. Why on earth would they be interested in auditioning me and why so last minute?'

'Calm down, Holly, you'll be fine. I overheard Maddie, the assistant producer of *On The Sofa*, talking to one of the main presenters while I was in the make-up room. Apparently the new producer, Richard Masters, is trying to stamp his mark on the programme by replacing their existing travel expert, Stuart Clapham, because he's a bit of a dinosaur and the ratings on that segment of the show are at rock bottom. Maddie had suggested a friend of hers for a screen test after the show finished this morning but she rang and cancelled at the last minute. Richard went on the warpath, threatening to fire people. Obviously Maddie was panicking because the recommendation had come from her. I just asked her if she'd heard of the Liberty Sands blog and she couldn't believe it when I told her I knew the girl who wrote it, and that she was young and beautiful.'

Holly blushed. 'Oh no,' she said. 'So they are expecting someone fifteen years younger than me, without wrinkles or eye bags the size of black bin liners. I'm just not sure I can do this, Philippe. Writing about travel is so different from talking about it into a camera, especially when you know there are millions of people watching. Did it ever occur to you that I might not want to be famous?'

'Everybody wants to be famous, Holly. You're panicking. Just be yourself and everyone will love you as much as I do. You know from your blog that hundreds of thousands of people already value your opinion on travel. The presenters will ask you the relevant questions and if you don't know the answer just say so. Honesty is always the best policy with the viewers at home. It's much more endearing than trying to make out you know about something when you don't.'

'Well, I'm here now so I suppose I might as well have a go or it will be a wasted journey.'

Philippe looked hurt. 'Well, not entirely wasted, at least you got to see me and maybe we could go for lunch after your screen test? If Harry's looking after Rosie you haven't got to dash back and I've actually got a rare afternoon off. There is just one thing. They are interested in having Liberty Sands as the travel expert, not Holly Wilson. Would that bother you?'

'No, of course it wouldn't bother me, but it might have an impact on my work for Soleil Resorts, after all, I am supposed to travel incognito.'

'If this comes off, maybe you wouldn't need to go on your monthly trips abroad, particularly now that you've got our daughter to consider. I'm not sure all the flying would be good for her at such a young age.'

Holly examined Philippe's face for a moment. Was that what this whole idea was about? Philippe didn't want his daughter carted off on regular long-haul flights to distant destinations? They weren't even a couple, in the proper sense of the word, and he was already trying to influence her decisions on their daughter's upbringing. Before she could respond, there was a knock on the door.

'Hello,' said a very tall, stunningly beautiful, African Caribbean woman. 'I'm Maddie. Philippe's told me all about you. Let's get you into make-up for a little touch-up. They're wrapping up the live show in ten minutes and they want to get the screen test done as quickly as possible after that so they can release the crew. I can't believe I'm actually talking to Liberty Sands. I love your blog. In fact, I've booked my next holiday to Thailand as a result of your recommendations.'

'No pressure there then,' muttered Holly under her breath, almost jogging to keep up with Maddie's long stride.

'Break a leg!' Philippe called out to her retreating back.

CHAPTER 3

Carol could hear people talking in hushed voices in the corridor outside her room. She was confused. She wasn't in her own bed. This one was very firm and had crisp white sheets and she felt warm, something she never did in her draughty old house. On numerous occasions the council had tried to persuade her to move out of her home, temporarily they always insisted, while they installed double-glazing, but Carol wasn't having any of that. She knew their game. Once they got her out of her three-bedroomed council house and into some pokey little flat they would find an excuse to make her stay there.

The volume of the voices was increasing as though the participants were in a heated discussion.

'She's too much for one person to manage. She needs to be institutionalised. It was only a bite on the hand this time. What if she had hidden a kitchen knife in her bed and had attacked you with that?'

'She's not violent. She just felt trapped and afraid. What kind of life would she have locked away and permanently on drugs to subdue her? I can't let that happen to her.'

'Why do you care? It's not as though she's family or anything and I've heard the way she speaks to you sometimes. I don't know how you put up with her. Hasn't she got any relatives that could care for her?'

'She's only got me. Her husband died years ago in a car crash and she rarely talks about her estranged daughter. What sort of person abandons a parent suffering from dementia?'

'You missed out two important words, Helen, "alcohol-induced" dementia.'

'Nobody knows that for sure.'

'True, but I think we all know the cause of her liver cirrhosis. It's a miracle she lasted this long with the amount she drinks and the length of time she's had the addiction.'

'Addiction is an illness. We're supposed to be trying to help Carol, not blame her.'

'She's brought this on herself. And don't go all "high and mighty" on me; you were just blaming the daughter for not being around but are you really in a position to judge? It's pretty dreadful growing up with a mother who's a drunk. Trust me, I know.'

'Helen, is that you?' Carol called out. 'Who are you talking to?'

The door opposite Carol's bed opened and a plumpish grey-haired woman in her late forties entered.

'It's just Mrs Ellery, your social worker. You gave us all quite a scare last night.'

Carol's forehead creased into a frown. 'What happened last night?'

A relieved expression crossed Helen's face. 'You had another fall. You tripped on your nightie and went headlong down the stairs.'

Carol stared vacantly at Helen for a moment trying to recall anything from the previous few hours. Her mind was blank. 'I want to go home now. I don't like it here it smells and,' she lowered her voice conspiratorially and indicated the tray of untouched food in front of her, 'I think they're trying to poison me.'

'Come on, Carol, you know that's not true. Everyone is worried about you because you don't eat enough. You're wasting away.'

'I don't like fat people. You're fat,' she said, accusingly. 'That's why I don't like you.'

Mrs Ellery had followed Helen into the room.

'I rest my case,' she said. 'She's rude and ungrateful. I'm sure we could get her sectioned under the Mental Health Act.'

'What's she saying, Helen? You won't let her hurt me, will you? Can we go home now?' she begged, reaching for Helen's hand.

Helen glared at the social worker. 'I'll go and find the doctor and see if we can take you home. Don't upset her,' she hissed at the younger woman, brushing past her to go in search of the nursing staff.

Carol tried to sit up in her bed and pull her knees into her chest to protect herself as she always had, but the tray table was in the way. She pulled the sheets tightly up to her chin instead, her eyes never leaving Mrs Ellery's face.

'Have you heard of euthanasia, Carol?' she asked, in a low menacing voice. 'They put animals to sleep when they are useless; it's a shame they don't do it with people too. Wouldn't you like to just go to sleep, Carol? To close your eyes and drift off, for ever? It would save a lot of money and paperwork. Maybe you should ask Helen to buy you some nice whisky and then take all your pills in one go? Think about it, Carol. Wouldn't that be the best thing for everybody?'

Carol's eyes were as big as saucers and her knuckles white from gripping the sheet. Perhaps this woman was right. What good was she to anyone? What good had she ever been? Even her own mother hadn't believed her when she had tried to tell her about the nocturnal visits from Uncle George.

CHAPTER 4

Holly could feel a trickle of sweat running down her spine. She wasn't sure if it was nerves or the heat from the bright studio lights but, either way, she was relieved that Tamsin, the make-up lady, had given her face a generous dusting of matte powder along with the rosy blusher, subtle eye make-up and coral lip gloss. Perched on the edge of the familiar mustard-yellow sofa, previously only viewed from the comfort of her duck-egg blue one at home, Holly caught a glimpse of herself on a television screen high on the studio wall and had to admit that Tamsin knew her craft. She had also been really kind, urging Holly to just relax and enjoy the experience.

'The camera is going to love you, and in television that's half the battle,' she had said, standing back to admire her handiwork.

The camera may love me but I'm not so sure Annabel does, Holly thought, glancing nervously at the morning show co-presenter who always seemed so friendly and approachable on TV.

'Do we have to wait for Simon?' Annabel asked tersely.

Holly glanced around the empty studio. 'I... erm...

guess not.'

'I wasn't talking to you,' Annabel snapped. 'I was asking the production team in the gallery but, by the lack of response, I'm guessing there's no one in there either. Look, I'm sorry. I didn't mean to be rude. It's been a hell of a morning and I have a lunch date. It's infuriating that Simon couldn't go another fifteen minutes without a cigarette. It's typical of him to keep everyone waiting. Have you done much telly work, Hannah?'

'It's Holly, actually, and no, I'm new to this. I'm not really sure how I got talked into coming today. I'm out of my depth; I should probably just go home.'

'Sorry to have kept you, Holly. This is Richard, the producer of the show,' a voice boomed from a small black speaker next to two more monitors on the studio floor. 'We were just having a look at you on camera and you've certainly passed that test. Simon's on his way down now so we'll get going in a couple of minutes. And Annabel… try and be civil.'

A pink stain coloured Annabel's cheeks. She put her hand over the small black microphone clipped to the lapel of her jacket and whispered, 'They're as thick as thieves, those two. Be careful, they try it on with every good-looking female on the show.'

It was Holly's turn to blush. Annabel was slim, blonde and leggy and at least fifteen years her junior. That was a massive compliment coming from her. 'Thanks for the warning,' she whispered back, taking Annabel's lead and covering her microphone, preventing the observers in the gallery from hearing their exchange.

Fifteen minutes later the audition was over. Holly was relieved but also elated. It had gone far better than she could have dreamed, particularly as she had seemingly found a new friend in Annabel who had gone out of her way to make her questions as specific as possible, to solicit the most descriptive and informative responses. As she unclipped her microphone, she gave Holly a surreptitious thumbs-up, before rushing off for her lunch date.

Maddie, who had been watching from behind the cameras, was also clearly impressed. 'You're a natural,' she said, as she led Holly up to the production gallery to meet Richard face to face.

Holly wasn't quite sure what she had imagined Richard would look like, but she was unprepared for the young, bearded man who was leaning against a huge desk filled with buttons and knobs, framed by eight television monitors that were all showing a still picture of her face from a variety of different angles. She could feel herself blushing.

'Holly, this is the producer of *On The Sofa*, Richard Masters.'

'Pleased to meet you,' she said, extending her hand.

Ignoring the gesture, he said, 'Hmmm, not bad,' while looking Holly up and down and making her feel as though he was undressing her with his eyes. 'Obviously you're a bit rough around the edges but I'm sure we could soon lick you into shape,' he added suggestively. 'Presumably you've worked with autocue and talkback?'

Before Holly could answer, Maddie interjected. 'We were a bit short of time today so we didn't bother with talkback.'

'Who is your agent? I'll give them a call this afternoon

and see if we can agree terms for a three-month probation period.'

Again it was Maddie who spoke. 'I've got all the details, Richard. I'll pop them up to the office when I've seen Holly out. Was there anything you wanted to ask Richard about the job, Holly?' she said, slowly shaking her head from side to side from her position behind the producer's right shoulder.

'Not really, except when would you be wanting me to start?'

'Don't tell me you're tied into a contract with someone else,' Richard barked. 'I hope you haven't been wasting my bloody time!'

'No, no, nothing like that.'

'Good. I can't stand time-wasters.'

'Richard can sort that out with your agent this afternoon, Holly,' Maddie said, propelling her out of the gallery. When they were safely out of earshot she said, 'I'm presuming you don't actually have an agent?'

Holly shook her head.

'I thought not and I didn't want that jumped-up arsehole trying to get you to do the job for peanuts.'

'But how am I going to find an agent by the time you need to give Richard some contact details?'

'I'm sure plenty of agents would jump at the chance to represent someone who has just landed a job on the nation's number one morning show, but time isn't on your side. If you want, we can ring my flatmate, Larry. He represents the girl who I'd originally suggested for the audition today, the one who blew us out at the last minute. If you two hit it off, I wouldn't be surprised if he gave her her marching orders. She's been getting in the papers for all the wrong reasons lately, falling out of nightclubs at all hours of the morning with traces of white powder around her nose. That's more than likely the reason she blew us out today. Stoned, high, drunk or hung-over. Take your pick.'

'Would he really be interested in representing me? I've got no experience and I have no clue about working with talkback or the technique for reading autocue?'

'It's not as difficult as you think. I can help a bit and Annabel seemed to warm to you after the frosty start. You'll be fine.'

'Why are you being so nice, Maddie? I hardly know you.'

'I could say I'm just a genuinely nice person and I want to help, but that wouldn't be entirely true. If I hadn't managed to find someone to fill the audition slot, Richard would probably have fired me, even though it wasn't my fault. It was a stroke of luck that sexy Philippe Marchant was on the show today and just happens to know *the* Liberty Sands. This might get me promoted,' Maddie said, laughing, 'and who knows, maybe even a date with Philippe. How do you two know each other?'

Holly was about to say that she and Philippe were an item but stopped herself, not wanting to jeopardise Maddie's offer of help. There would be plenty of time to come clean about her involvement with Philippe once she had secured the job, but she couldn't help wondering if he had given Maddie any reason for her obvious interest in him.

'Our paths have crossed in the publishing world,' she replied, truthfully. 'I hope I can live up to your expectations, Maddie, and, believe me, I won't forget this.'

CHAPTER 5

'Choo choo. Here comes the train into the tunnel,' Harry said, moving a pink plastic spoon, laden with mashed banana, in the direction of his baby sister's mouth. Rosie obligingly opened her mouth and then banged her plump hand on the tray of her high chair in appreciation. 'Here comes another one,' Harry said, scraping the remnants of the sweet fruit from Rosie's bowl as the front door slammed. 'In here, Mum,' he called. 'Rosie's finishing her tea. How did it go?' he asked, although one look at Holly's smiling face was answer enough.

'I'm in a state of shock, Harry. The producer of the show really liked me and seemed totally unconcerned by my lack of experience. They've offered me a three-month trial. It's ridiculous money.'

'Congratulations, Mum,' Harry said, wrapping his arms around her and squeezing her tightly. 'Don't worry about the money, the experience is invaluable and anyway, I'm sure they'll offer you a raise when they realise how good you are.'

Holly pulled away from her son, unclipped Rosie's

harness and started dancing around the room. 'When I said ridiculous, I didn't mean it was low. I just had a phone call from my new agent, I'll tell you about him in a minute,' she added, seeing Harry's incredulous expression. 'For the three months, it's more money than two years' worth of trips for Soleil, and that's only working three Friday mornings a month,' she trilled. 'I can't believe this is happening to me, and all thanks to Philippe. We should celebrate, Harry.'

'Something tells me you already have. Was your lunch with Philippe a liquid one by any chance?'

Holly stopped twirling, much to Harry's relief as he was fearful that his mother was about to be covered in regurgitated banana. 'We only had one glass of champagne each with lunch. Philippe wanted to buy a bottle but I don't like to encourage him to drink and besides it went straight to my head. It's the first alcoholic drink I've had since the champagne at Rosie's christening. I felt so guilty drinking while I was still feeding her, even though it was only a sip, but now she prefers the bottle to me, I think I deserve a celebratory drink. We can share a bottle of bubbly after Rosie's gone to bed. Do you want to pop to the shops while I get changed into something more comfortable for Rosie's play- and bathtime? I can't wait to tell Robert. I know he'll be so happy for me, or should I say us? It's funny, isn't it? Since meeting Robert and Rosemary in Mauritius, everything seems to finally be going our way.'

Harry didn't want to burst his mum's bubble of happiness by reminding her of all the sadness and despair she had also experienced in the previous year. It wouldn't hurt for her to wear her rose-tinted glasses for a little longer, he thought. 'Any preference of brand?'

Holly giggled. 'I have no idea, but I want the real thing, not sparkling wine or prosecco. It has to be champagne! Maybe we should ask Robert's opinion? He knows everything about wine. Come on, Harry, let's ring him now.'

The phone was answered on the third ring, 'Hello, Robert Forrester's phone.'

'Oh, hello. Is Robert there?' Holly asked, surprised that anyone but the man himself would be answering the phone.

'He's just popped out for a few minutes. Can I take a message and ask him to call back? Or you could try his mobile.'

'No worries, I'll try him later. Would you tell him that Holly rang, please?'

'Holly, hello. I didn't recognise your voice. It's Nick. How are you?'

Holly could feel the colour slowly rising into her cheeks. She hadn't seen Nick since they had all enjoyed lunch together at Robert's house shortly after Christmas but she had occasionally caught herself thinking about him.

'Nick... I didn't recognise your voice either. We're all fine. Harry's home for Easter, but you probably already knew that, and Rosie's as sweet as ever. She's started pulling her knees under her when she's lying on her tummy. I think she's trying to crawl. And me, well, I've just been offered a job on television,' she blurted out. 'That's why I was ringing Robert, to tell him my amazing news and ask him if he can recommend a champagne to celebrate. Any thoughts?'

'Well, I'm not exactly a connoisseur but, for what it's

worth, Bollinger is the best-tasting one that I've tried. It's perfect timing too. You'll have to share the bottle with Harry. Robert finally signed the contract for the redevelopment of the Philmore Hotel this afternoon, after all the negotiations over budgets and timescale. He was going to ring Harry later to tell him. I'm so pleased for you both. What television programme are you going to be on?'

'I don't suppose you have much time for daytime television, Nick. It's a programme called *On The Sofa*. I'm going to be their new travel features presenter, at least they are going to try me out for three months. It's crazy really, I've never been on TV before, nor wanted to be if I'm honest, but Philippe recommended me and I passed the audition. Sorry if I sound a bit gushy but I'm still on cloud nine.'

'And so you should be. It's the top morning show isn't it? You're right, I'm not a regular viewer of daytime TV but even I know that. Philippe? He's Rosie's dad isn't he? I didn't mean to exclude him from sharing the champagne, but you didn't mention he was there.'

'He's not. It's just the three of us and Rosie's a bit young for bubbly.'

'Right.' There was a slightly awkward pause before Nick spoke again, 'Hold on a minute, Holly, I think that's Robert's car. I'll go and hurry him up. It was nice talking to you again and good luck with the new job. Say hi to Harry for me.'

'Will do, Nick. It was nice to talk to you again too...' she began to say, but the sound of the phone being placed on a hard surface suggested that Nick was no longer listening.

CHAPTER 6

There hadn't been any total memory lapses since Carol had been released from hospital two weeks earlier. The bruising on her cheekbone and forehead had faded from a lurid purple to a dull mustard, but apart from that there was no evidence of the recent fall down the stairs. If anything, Carol seemed more alert than usual and was making a determined effort not to drink at all, even refusing the small measure of whisky that Helen normally offered her in her hot milk drink at bedtime. She was taking all the vitamin supplements that Helen lined up next to her plate of toast, or bowl of porridge, at breakfast and was managing to eat the small portions of food presented to her at every meal. There had been another change too. She had refused point-blank to allow Mrs Ellery into the house following her hospital stay. There were no histrionics, she had simply told Helen to ring the council and ask for someone else to be assigned to her.

'Did she upset you, Carol?' Helen had probed. 'If she did, we'll file a complaint.'

'No, I just don't like her,' Carol replied, and refused to

say anything else on the subject.

Her days had slipped back into the routine that Helen had established when she had moved into the house nine months previously. Carol hadn't wanted anyone living with her, treating her like a baby, but her choice was that or being moved into a nursing home. It was the lesser of two evils and Carol had planned, in her more lucid moments, to make Helen's life such a living hell that she wouldn't stay for more than a few weeks. But Helen had stayed. No matter how awful Carol was, spitting at her and calling her vile names when she refused to let her drink, the younger woman stayed calm and patient, explaining repeatedly what the doctor had told her when she had applied to be Carol's live-in carer. 'If you don't stop drinking you'll be dead within a year or, worse still, you'll live out your days in a vegetative state, not recognising anyone or remembering anything.'

'Why would I care?' she had railed. 'I've got nothing and no one to live for anyway. I'd rather be dead. Why can't you just leave me alone you interfering busybody? Why can't you understand? I don't want to remember things, that's why I started drinking in the first place. Just piss off back to where you've come from.'

If Helen was upset by Carol's behaviour or language she never let it show and gradually the verbal abuse lessened and the two were able to coexist in relative harmony.

Each day, after breakfast, if the weather allowed, they walked to the local shopping precinct to buy groceries. Helen insisted that the fresh air and exercise would do Carol good and she had to admit she felt better for getting out from the confines of her house which had begun to feel like a prison. Before Helen's arrival, Carol's only company, apart from periodic visits from social workers, had been her television. She would switch it on the moment she came downstairs in the morning and it stayed on until she went to bed at night, or sometimes through the night if she had been drinking heavily and was lying comatose on the sofa. Helen rationed her time in front of the TV, instead encouraging her to talk about her life or help with small domestic chores, but she always allowed her to enjoy her elevenses, a cup of milky coffee and a digestive biscuit, watching her favourite show *On The Sofa* after they got back from their morning walk.

That morning, as Helen was bringing the tray with their hot drinks through from the kitchen, Carol started shouting at the television. 'No... why would you do that? Why do you have to change things? I like Stuart, he's handsome.'

'What's wrong, Carol?' Helen asked, pushing the door open with her foot.

Carol didn't reply. She was staring at the screen, transfixed. 'They're lying,' she suddenly blurted out. 'That's not her name,' she said, pointing to the words on the bottom of the screen.

Helen put the tray down and glanced at the TV. The caption read: *Liberty Sands, travel expert and blogger.*

'They're always getting things like that wrong these days,' she said, handing Carol her mug of coffee. 'Do you remember last week when they captioned that political activist as the fashion editor of *HiYa* magazine? It's a wonder they don't get sued. Anyway, isn't Stuart Clapham their travel expert? Is he away on holiday?'

'Shut up,' Carol shrieked, 'I'm trying to listen. Just stop talking!' Carol was working herself up into an agitated state. 'It's her. I wasn't sure until I heard her speak,' Carol said, her voice incredulous.

'Who do you think it is?'

'I don't *think*, you stupid woman, I know. I'd know that bitch anywhere. That's my daughter Holly,' she shouted, launching her coffee mug at the television.

The china mug broke on contact with the television screen, depositing what was left of the contents on to the smiling face of Liberty Sands as she talked about the perfect time to travel to the Caribbean. Helen looked from Carol to the screen and back to Carol who was hugging herself, rocking back and forward, and muttering, 'Leave me alone, leave me alone...'

'How can you be so sure it's your daughter?' Helen asked, gently. 'You told me you haven't seen her in over twenty years since she walked out. She won't look anything like you remember her.'

'Some things you never forget,' Carol said, shuddering. 'She looks like him.'

'Like who?'

'Her father. She has the same brown curly hair and those dark green eyes. Like two peas in a pod they were. They were always doing things together and excluding me.' Carol had a pained look on her face. 'She tried to steal him from me, you know, but he chose me. That's why she killed him.'

'I thought you said your husband died in a car crash? Was your daughter driving the car?'

Seemingly oblivious to the question, Carol said, 'She killed him, just to spite me and now she's laughing at me.'

They both turned to look at the television but the travel slot had finished and the show was on a commercial break.

'I like those biscuits, can we buy some?' Carol asked, her voice back to normal, as though the events of the previous five minutes hadn't happened.

'We'll have a look in the Co-op when we're out tomorrow. Let me get you a fresh mug of coffee.'

Carol spotted the broken china on the faded rug in front of the fireplace. 'You should be more careful, Helen, that was my favourite mug.'

'I'm sorry, Carol, it just slipped out of my hand. I'll buy you a new one. You sit back and relax and I'll get this mess cleared up.'

CHAPTER 7

Holly was shaking as she made her way back towards the dressing room. Although she had been dreadfully nervous at her audition, it was nothing compared to the terror of being introduced to the British public as the replacement for the much-loved, although slightly past it, Stuart Clapham. To think that two million pairs of eyes had been scrutinising her. Her mouth had felt like the Sahara Desert and the lights seemed much brighter today, causing her to blink a lot. She had tried to remember everything Annabel had told her about reading the autocue without allowing her eyes to travel from left to right but she was convinced she had failed miserably. The only saving grace was that the director had not spoken to her at all via her newly moulded earpiece while she was live to the nation, allowing her to concentrate on answering the questions fired at her by Annabel and Simon. In the space of five minutes she had developed a huge admiration for the two television presenters sat on the sofa opposite her who made their job look so easy. How did I ever think I could do this? she thought, pushing open the door to the dressing room.

'Surprise!'

Holly stopped in her tracks. She had expressly told Harry that she didn't want any fuss and he had agreed to watch from home. Why then was he stood in front of her, holding a huge bunch of flowers, with his university pal Amy on one side and on the other Robert cradling her baby daughter?

'You were awesome, Mum,' Harry said, his voice full of pride as he wrapped his arms around her, holding the flowers to one side so as not to crush them.

'Don't you mean awful?' Holly asked. 'I think maybe your opinion is a little biased, seeing as you're a blood relative.'

'Well, I'm not, and I have to agree with Harry that you were marvellous, much better than your senile predecessor who always sounded slightly drunk to my ears,' Robert said, handing over a smiling Rosie.

'You're just being kind, Robert, I can't imagine you're a regular viewer of On The Sofa. Is Philippe here too?'

There was a moment of silence before Robert replied, 'No, he sends his love. I think he had a radio interview or something. He's going to try and join us for lunch though.'

Holly could read her friend like an open book. He was a terrible liar, which made him even more endearing when he tried. Despite requesting that none of her friends or family turn up at the television studios she was secretly pleased that they had, making the disappointment of Philippe not being there more acute.

'I've followed the show on Twitter, Holly,' Amy said, touching the screen of her iPhone, 'and there are loads of tweets, most of them really positive. Listen to these: "Easier on the eye and the ear than the old guy... Seems to know her stuff... Refreshing new approach... Actually listened to the presenter's questions..." I think you can safely say you've created a good impression. I'm so pleased for you,' she said, hugging Holly and Rosie at the same time.

'Thanks for coming, Amy. I can't believe Harry organised this behind my back but I'm glad he did.'

Holly allowed herself to relax. Clearly the way she had felt and the way she had come across to the viewers at home were totally different. Perhaps feeling nervous in the world of television was a good thing.

'I'm just relieved to have the first one out of the way – always assuming there will be more. According to Maddie, Richard, the show's new producer, is hiring and firing at will at the moment to flex his muscles and show who is boss. He's the one I need to have impressed. I have to wait until the show is finished and then go and have a debrief meeting. I'm almost as nervous about that as going on TV. Do you really think I did okay?'

'Now you're just fishing for compliments. Joke, Mum,' Harry said, as Holly started to protest. 'We'll go and wait for you in the reception area downstairs. Maybe we'll get a decent table at the restaurant now that you're a telly star,' he added.

Forty-five minutes later there was a knock at the dressing room door. It was Maddie.

'Well done, my little protégée,' she said, smiling. 'You were every bit as good as I knew you would be. Richard wants to see you in his office for a debrief. He seems pretty happy but you never know with him. Just don't let him bully you, okay?'

'Yes, boss. Listen, my family and some friends are down in reception. They're taking me out for a celebratory lunch. I don't suppose you'd like to join us?'

'I've got a few phone calls to make for tomorrow's show but I could always come back and do them later, provided you haven't plied me with too much champagne. Is your friend Philippe going to be there?'

'Maybe. Look, I should probably have mentioned this before. Philippe and I are sort of an item. He's my baby's father, but it was an unplanned pregnancy when we didn't know each other very well. We hit a bit of a rough patch a few months back but we both want to have another go at making things work.'

'Right. Well, I hope it works out for you both, you make a lovely couple,' Maddie said, her voice lacking conviction. 'He hasn't got an even more handsome brother has he?' she added, the twinkle returning to her eye. 'Maybe a couple of years younger?'

'No, he's an only child, like me,' Holly replied. 'You know, it's funny. I would never have wished for any child of mine to have a solitary upbringing but somehow I seem to have managed it twice, unless Philippe and I can make a go of things, if you get my drift,' she said, blushing furiously.

'Don't be embarrassed, we all have sex you know. My parents must have been at it like rabbits. There are seven of us, five girls and two boys, and we lived in a three-bedroomed flat so I had to share a room with my four sisters. I can't tell you how many times I've wished I was an only child just for a bit of peace and quiet.'

'It's not all it's cracked up to be. It can be very lonely,

particularly if you don't have a great relationship with your mum.'

'I struck gold on that front. My mum is my rock and my best friend. We'd better go or Richard will get arsy, he hates being kept waiting. And, on second thoughts, I think I'll skip the lunch invitation if you don't mind. With him on the warpath I don't want to give him a reason to fire me.'

Was that the real reason? Holly wondered, following Maddie down the corridor.

CHAPTER 8

'Nice of you to join me,' Jo said, sarcastically, tapping the Cartier watch on her left wrist.

Philippe landed a perfunctory kiss on her cheek before settling himself on the plush velvet chair opposite her, similar in colour to the glass of Merlot his editor from Ripped Publishing had just placed on the pristine white tablecloth.

'I thought we agreed on twelve thirty,' she persisted. 'Knowing your total disregard for punctuality, I arrived fifteen minutes late, but this,' she said, tapping her wrist watch again, 'is borderline rude. I hope you're not this late for your radio and television interviews? It wouldn't do to piss the media off.'

'You're lucky I'm here at all. The traffic coming in to London on the M4 from my radio interview in the back of beyond was appalling. Did you organise it deliberately so that I would miss Holly's debut on *On The Sofa* this morning?'

'Oh, was that today? Sorry, I'm a bit too busy negotiating six-figure sums for ungrateful writers. It would appear that daytime TV has slipped under my radar.'

Philippe observed his editor. She had returned to being the hard-headed, hard-hearted businesswoman since her brief fling with Geoff from the bookshop in Bath. 'And I suppose it was coincidental that you called this lunch meeting for today when we've barely set eyes on each other in months. I can't believe you're so jealous of my and Holly's relationship.'

Jo raised her eyes from the leather-bound menu. 'Your private life is of no interest to me except when it interferes with your writing. You're so busy playing happy families that I've not even had a sniff of an idea for your third book.'

'Did you ever stop to consider that it might be more to do with the relentless promotional work you've got me doing? There can't be a local radio station or women's magazine anywhere in the British Isles that hasn't interviewed me. I'm tired, Jo, and when I'm tired I can't be creative.'

'You're right, Phil. Maybe you should do what you did for the last book and just take off on your own for a few months?'

'Nice try, but if I do go away anywhere Holly and Rosie will be coming with me.'

'Really? Won't that be a tad difficult now that you've landed her a weekly slot on TV?'

'For someone who professes to have no interest in Holly, you seem to know a lot about what her new job entails.'

Jo could kick herself for revealing the extent of her interest in Holly's new job. She had been stunned when Philippe had first told her that Holly was the secret travel blogger writing under the pseudonym of Liberty Sands.

She had been an avid reader of the blog since Alice, her PA, had mentioned that it had helped her and her boyfriend select the perfect holiday destination. Even though there was little point in Jo reading it, as she very rarely took time off and only ever travelled abroad for business, there was something engagingly honest about the blog and she had to grudgingly admit that Holly had a real flair for the written word. She was having an internal battle with herself. Now that Holly was set to become a TV personality, there was a brilliant opportunity to sign her up to write a travel book but Jo just couldn't bring herself to make the suggestion to Holly, despite her fears that another publishing house might steal her from under Ripped's nose. She hadn't passed any manuscripts Holly's way for copy-editing since the evening at Mosimann's restaurant in Knightsbridge. She kept making the excuse that with a new baby to look after, Holly wouldn't have the time or concentration levels required to edit a manuscript, but Jo knew that the real reason was plain, old-fashioned jealousy.

'It was just an assumption, Phil,' Jo said, regaining her composure. 'I wouldn't imagine that a television company would bother to train a complete novice for a one-off appearance.'

'Well, you're almost right as it happens, she's contracted to appear three Fridays a month so that she can still fulfil her blogging obligations. Actually, maybe that's the answer. I could just tag along on her next trip. I think she said she was going to Mexico, or was it Cuba? You know, the more I think of it the more I like the idea. I'll find out the dates and give them to Alice at the office so she can keep my diary clear. Thanks, Jo,' Philippe said, unable to resist smirking.

'So long as you get some writing done, I couldn't care less,' Jo lied. 'Are you ready to order?'

CHAPTER 9

Robert and Holly walked along one of the many paths in Battersea Park in the warmth of the spring sunshine, pushing a sleeping Rosie in her pram. Holly envied her baby daughter. After an early start, a highly stressful television debut and a fairly alcoholic lunch, all she wanted to do was curl up in a ball and go to sleep, but that wasn't an option. It was Robert who had suggested taking a stroll in the park, allegedly to give Rosie a breath of fresh air after the confines of the television studio and the restaurant, but Holly knew that wasn't the real reason. He clearly wanted to spend a little more time with the closest thing to family that he had following the death of his wife, Rosemary. It would be the first anniversary of her death in a few weeks and Holly had made sure that her trips abroad for Soleil Resorts wouldn't clash with it so that she would be around to spend time with him.

'I was just thinking how proud of you Rosemary would have been. A new baby and a new career all in the space of a few months. All you need now is a new man.'

'A new man?' Holly said, raising her eyebrows. 'Do you

know something I don't about Philippe's no show today?'

'Sorry, that came out totally wrong,' Robert said, in a fluster. 'What I meant was, it would be the icing on the cake to see you settled in a relationship.'

'I know, but I don't want to rush things. There is still so much I don't know about Philippe like, for example, why he didn't come to lunch today after telling you he would try. I'd have thought he would want to celebrate with us, particularly as I got the job on his recommendation. I just don't understand him sometimes.'

'When I spoke to him last night, he said he was going to try and get out of his lunch appointment if he got back to London early enough to make it to the restaurant for one. He probably got held up in traffic and thought it would be too late to join us.'

'There are these quirky new devices called mobile phones, Robert,' Holly said, her voice loaded with sarcasm. 'Surely he could have rung or text to say he couldn't make it?'

'You're forgetting; it was supposed to be a surprise having us all turn up at the studios. I wouldn't have mentioned Philippe at all if you hadn't asked me a direct question.'

'I suppose you're right, but I would still have thought he could have sent a text to ask me how it went. Maybe I just expect too much from him. Who did you say his lunch date was with?'

'I didn't. And I definitely wouldn't call it a date. He was meeting his editor. It's the first time they've been face to face since the night Rosie was born. He told me how vile she was to you. If anything had happened to my little angel because of her,' Robert said, reaching into the pram to tuck Rosie's hand back under the blanket, 'I'd have… I'd have…'

'Trust me, you'd have been behind me and Harry in the queue. No wonder Philippe couldn't ring; she'd probably confiscated his phone. Anyway, let's stop talking about Jo, I don't want her spoiling my special day. Are you pleased about the Philmore?'

'Amazed, if I'm honest. Your boy came up with some pretty extravagant renovation ideas and the hotel have agreed to most of them. The only thing left to finalise is a start date. I've tried to delay things a bit so that it won't clash with Harry's exams but at least now we've got Nick on board, he can get the ball rolling. It's their project, I'm much too busy with plans for a hotel refurbishment in Hong Kong.'

'I'm glad Harry's going to be working with someone as experienced as Nick, he'll be able to learn so much and you're right, it will take the pressure off him until he's finished his finals.'

'Nick's a genuinely nice chap. He drops by far more than he needs to just for a chat or a coffee. He's another one I'd like to see happily settled down.'

Holly shot Robert a sidelong glance. 'Is he seeing anyone?' she asked, casually.

'Not that I know of. He's still licking his wounds after the divorce, I think. What's going on with those two?' he asked, indicating Harry and Amy, who were animatedly chatting fifty yards ahead of them on the path.

'Absolutely nothing. I guess I hoped that they may get together when Amy split from Jack but Harry doesn't seem to see her as anything but a friend.'

'But they are so perfect for each other, any fool can

see that.'

'Robert,' Holly said, a note of warning in her voice, 'resist the urge to meddle.'

'I will, I promise. It's just that having waited so long to find my soulmate, finding out that our paths had crossed before and we'd missed the opportunity fate presented us with, and then losing her so soon, still plays on my mind. I hate the thought of anyone, particularly people I care about, letting the chance of happiness slip through their fingers.'

'They're still very young, Robert, they've got their whole lives ahead of them.'

'They are, but you not so.'

'Thanks for reminding me! I can't believe I'll be forty in June. I certainly don't feel it, even after the occasional sleepless night.'

'You don't look it either.'

'There I go again, unintentionally fishing for compliments,' Holly said, a familiar flush rising into her cheeks.

'Well, I'm happy to pay them to you when they are so richly deserved. I just wish Philippe would make his move before you get tired of waiting.'

Holly stopped walking and turned to face Robert. 'It's not him, it's me. Do you remember the present from Tiffany's that Philippe gave me at Christmas? It wasn't a pen, it was a diamond engagement ring. I'd asked him not to rush things but he didn't listen. I fell totally and hopelessly in love with a man I barely knew and now I'm wondering whether the differences between us are insurmountable.'

'What do you mean, Holly? Philippe worships the

ground you walk on. When you're in the room he never takes his eyes off you. Surely love is the most important thing?'

'Half of me says it is. When we're together, snuggled on the sofa watching a film, with Rosie fast asleep in her cot upstairs, I feel content. Happy. Complete, even. But then he'll make a comment like he did the other day, suggesting that now I've got the job at *On The Sofa*, I should give up travelling for Soleil because it would be better for Rosie. I don't want to feel controlled. I've spent so many years making all my own decisions, I'm not sure I would be able to let someone else do it for me, even if I wanted to.'

'I can see that, Holly. But he does have a point about Rosie. What will happen when she's a bit older? You wouldn't be allowed to take her out of school, you know.'

'By that stage I will have satisfied my wanderlust. I guess what I'm saying is that I want to make that choice, not have it forced on me. And then, of course, there's the drinking. I don't want to spend another moment of my life in the company of an alcoholic. I've seen, first hand, how it ruins lives, including that of the addict. I can't go there, Robert, truly I can't, no matter how much I love Philippe.'

'Hey, you two,' Harry called, from a hundred yards down the path, 'hurry up. I want to try and beat the rush-hour traffic.'

Robert placed his hand over Holly's on the handle of the pram and squeezed it. 'Do you want me to quietly suggest to Philippe that he joins Alcoholics Anonymous for his own good?'

'No, Robert,' Holly said, quickening her pace to catch

up with Harry and Amy, 'he has to decide for himself what is most important in his life. We all do.'

CHAPTER 10

Helen was hanging the washing out on Saturday morning, in the warm April sunshine, and finding it hard to believe that only three weeks previously Carol's back garden had been six inches deep in snow. She had been fearful that the daffodil bulbs she had lovingly planted in November, that already had six-inch shoots showing when the cold snap hit, would have perished beneath their icy blanket. She needn't have worried. The golden trumpets bobbed around in the light breeze and clusters of purple, white and yellow crocuses brightened up the newly created border. It had taken Helen several weeks during the previous summer to cut back the rampant brambles and dig out nettles and thistles to reveal a decent-sized space. There were no flowers or shrubs, just patchy clumps of grass and a small paved area made slimy by moss. Each afternoon, when Carol was having a nap to make up for her disturbed nights, Helen weeded and mowed and planted. It was still a long way from perfect but at least now it was a pleasant place to encourage Carol to sit and enjoy a cup of tea on warm days. Anything to get her out of the drab house, which

Helen was yet to tackle.

Gardening was Helen's passion. For twenty years she had nurtured the plants in the oasis of calm she had created at the back of her marital home in Beeston, near the Queen's Medical Centre where she worked as a nurse. It was the only thing she had been sad to leave when she handed the keys to the bailiff on the morning she was evicted. Helen could still remember the humiliation she felt walking down the front garden path and closing the white picket gate behind her for the final time. She refused to cry, there had been enough tears, and besides she wouldn't give her neighbours, some of whom she knew would be watching from behind their net curtains, the satisfaction. Head held high, she climbed into the hired Ford transit van, containing the sparse possessions she had been allowed to keep, and drove off down the road to an uncertain future, thankful that her parents hadn't lived to see the disgrace she was suffering.

Helen had never had the slightest inkling that something was terribly wrong with her marriage. Her husband Graeme had seemed such a good man. His job as an area sales manager for a pharmaceutical company kept him away from home a lot but she had no reason to suspect that he was already married when he had swept her off her feet in a whirlwind romance. The evening he hadn't returned from one of his frequent business trips, Helen had been beside herself with worry. She reported him missing and within days the police had located him in a hospital in Birmingham, following a heart attack. He regained consciousness briefly, and apologised to the two women he had loved, before another massive heart attack two days later claimed his life. Both his wives were at his bedside.

The shock of his death and discovering he had another wife paled into insignificance when the level of debt he had got himself into, supporting two homes, was revealed. Helen had very little in the way of savings and it soon became apparent that she would lose her home because of her inability to pay the mortgage. She didn't care; she no longer wanted to live in a house that had harboured such a huge and devastating lie.

Her friends were kind, allowing her to sleep on their couches or in their spare bedrooms until she had scraped enough money together for a deposit to rent a flat. It was small but it was home. The major drawback was that it had no garden so Helen needed another hobby to fill her spare time. A friend was about to pay a company to make her family tree so, as a thank you for letting her stay with them, Helen volunteered to do it for nothing. It was the start of a new passion, one that would eventually turn Helen's world upside down for a second time.

'Helen, are you out there?' Carol called.

'Just coming,' she replied. 'It's a beautiful day, why don't we hop on a bus down to Trent Bridge and go for a walk along the river.'

'Yes, I'd like that. I could show you the house where I grew up.'

Carol had no idea that Helen already knew exactly where the house was.

An hour later, the two women stepped off the bus on the city side of Trent Bridge. Helen linked her arm through Carol's and flinched at the near skeletal feel through the thin fabric of her lightweight blue jacket. Despite congratulating Carol on finishing all her meals since her last stay in hospital, Helen knew that the tiny bird-size portions weren't enough to build up the older woman's strength, but at least she was eating and had stopped drinking completely, for the time being.

'We won't go too far,' Helen said, guiding Carol towards the path next to the river, away from the traffic on Victoria Embankment. The sunlight was twinkling on the water and glinting off the droplets that fell from the oars of the rowers practising near the far bank. The men were in vest tops and shorts and with each smooth even stroke, every sinew of every muscle was engaged. It was mesmeric. Four pairs of oars sliced into the water, lifted, twisted and dipped again to propel the boat forward at pace.

'I don't really like the water much,' Carol said, suddenly. 'I went on a pleasure boat once and I dropped my doll Margaret over the side. Daddy tried to rescue her for me but she floated away out of reach, her beautiful lace dress ruined and her face down in the water like she had drowned. I had nightmares about it for months afterwards. I kept waking up screaming, unable to breathe because I thought the water was filling my lungs. Mummy was so kind at first, but eventually she got cross with me for waking her up in the night. I think that's why she wouldn't listen to me when I told her about Uncle George,' she added, an anguished look in her eyes.

'Uncle George?' Helen probed, gently. 'I'll listen, if you want to tell me about him.'

Carol didn't reply, as though she hadn't heard the question. Instead she said, 'I like Nottingham. I don't know why anyone would ever want to move away. It's got the castle and the river and Robin Hood, of course. Have you always lived in Nottingham, Helen?'

It was the first time in nine months that Carol had asked any questions about her past. Helen was anxious to steer the conversation back to Carol but knew she needed to satisfy the older woman's curiosity. 'Yes. I was born and raised here. I grew up in Arnold and then moved to Beeston, to be closer to the hospital.'

'Were you a nurse then? Before you became a carer?'

'Yes, for the best part of thirty years. I started as a student nurse and moved up through the ranks. I used to love my job but it's changed in recent times. For me it was a vocation, a need to help and care for people when they were at their most vulnerable. I might be wrong, but I'm not sure that's the motivation anymore. Everything, in all walks of life, seems to revolve around money, not that they pay nurses enough in my opinion.'

'Is that why you left, because they weren't paying you enough? Do you get more looking after me?'

'No,' Helen smiled. 'I took a pay cut to come and look after you.'

'Then why did you do it? I wasn't very nice to you at the beginning was I?'

'That's an understatement, but it must have been difficult for you to have someone move into your home and tell you what to do, even though I was only trying to help. I don't blame you for the things you said, I would probably have done the same in your situation.'

'You didn't answer my question.'

'It was just the right time to leave. I'd been doing some specialist nursing qualifications,' she said, choosing her words carefully, 'and just decided I'd rather do it in the community rather than on the wards.'

'I'm glad you did,' Carol said, taking Helen by surprise. It was the first time she had ever expressed anything close to gratitude and Helen didn't know how to respond.

'We should probably turn back now. I don't want you getting over-tired.'

'But I didn't show you my old house yet. Come on,' she said, reaching for Helen's hand, her eyes shining with excitement, 'I know a short cut through the Memorial Gardens.'

The two of them crossed the wide road, flanked on each side by tall trees with their newly unfurled leaves, to where two low metal gates marked the entrance to the gardens. Moments before, Carol had seemed in a hurry but now she stood in front of the gates as though they were a barrier that she wasn't permitted to cross.

'Shall we go in, Carol?'

'Yes. I bet he'll be waiting for us by the lily pond,' she said, pushing the gate open.

Before Helen could ask who might be waiting for them by the pond, Carol had scurried off down the gravel path between the trees and neatly planted flowerbeds. She was moving quite fast, like someone half her age, and Helen could feel perspiration forming on her top lip as she had to quicken her pace to keep up. After a couple of minutes, they emerged into an open space with a sizeable pond encased in raised stone walls. At one end the impressive War Memorial towered above them and at the other an imperious looking statue of Queen Victoria was oblivious to their presence.

Carol was looking puzzled. 'What happened to the

water lilies?'

Helen looked into the less than clean water of the pond, empty apart from discarded cigarette butts and sweet wrappers. 'Maybe they died?' she ventured.

Carol ignored her comment. 'And where's Daddy? He should be here by now,' she said, looking from end to end of the pond like a tennis umpire, her voice trembling. 'Unless… yes, that's it, he'll have gone to buy ice creams. We'll go and wait for him by the giant weeping willow.' She was off again, moving at speed with Helen several paces behind her.

Helen was now beginning to wonder at the wisdom of bringing Carol to a place which had clearly evoked such vivid memories of her childhood that she had been transported back there. Ahead, Carol had stopped again at a fork in the path. She was looking anxiously from left to right.

'Daddy,' she called out in a small, shrill voice, 'where are you?'

Tears were starting to well up in Carol's eyes. Somehow Helen had to keep her calm until she returned to the present day. 'Perhaps he thought he'd missed us and has gone home?'

'Who?' Carol asked.

CHAPTER 11

Maddie turned the key in her front door and closed it behind her, flicking the deadlock and engaging the safety chain. It was force of habit. The tiny bedsit she had moved into when she left home at sixteen had been in a very rundown part of West Kensington, where break-ins were an everyday occurrence. She had learned her lesson the hard way when she had gone back to her room after taking a shower in the bathroom she shared with six other tenants to discover that she had forgotten to lock her door. Luckily, the only thing missing was her handbag with all its contents, which, although an inconvenience, was a real let off.

Throwing her Michael Kors bag on to the designer sofa and kicking off her Jimmy Choo's, she allowed herself a smile. The bag that had been stolen twelve years ago had cost her three pounds from a market stall. Her monthly rent then had been less than she had paid for her current handbag. She'd come a long way from her humble beginnings and climbed the career ladder quickly. She was aware that people talked about her behind her back, suggesting that she had got to her position via the casting couch, but she shrugged it off. Maddie never slept with anyone she worked with, regardless of their importance within the company. Middle-aged executives, whose wives no longer wanted to have sex with them, might flatter and charm other young co-workers into their bed, but Maddie was immune. Once a brief fling was over it was easy to have someone made redundant because their position 'no longer existed'. It was not a risk Maddie was prepared to take. She wanted to be the youngest executive producer in television and nothing was going to stand in her way. She didn't do relationships, but she did like sex. She had a strict rule only to sleep with men who were already in a relationship. That way both parties understood it was sex without ties.

Maddie poured herself a generous glass of chilled Chardonnay and reached into her bag for her phone. Scrolling through the numbers she paused at Philippe Marchant's name. She liked Holly a lot but that was business and this was pleasure. Now that she knew Philippe was in a relationship she was very tempted to give him a call. The sexy light green eyes and the occasional hint of a French accent on certain words were an intoxicating mix. She crossed the plush white carpet and stood sipping her wine, gazing out of the sliding glass doors at the murky-looking River Thames as it made its way lazily towards the estuary. Her flatmate Larry was away overnight in Newcastle, having answered an urgent call from a client who was experiencing stage fright for the first time in his thirty-year career. Really, Maddie thought, the job of an agent sometimes bears striking similarities to that of a babysitter.

She tapped the side of her now half empty glass,

thoughtfully. If what Holly had said about taking things slowly meant what she thought it meant, Philippe would be gagging for sex. In a way she would be doing Holly a favour, satisfying his sexual urges with no emotional involvement and he could always say no. She touched the screen of her phone and waited for a couple of rings before it went to voicemail.

'Oh hi, Philippe,' she purred, 'this is Maddie, from *On The Sofa*. It appears that you and I are near neighbours. I wondered if maybe you're at a loose end this evening and fancy a bit of company? We could order in a takeaway at mine if you fancy it. Let me know, before I slip into my onesie and resort to a microwave dinner.'

Maddie didn't own a onesie but she thought it made it sound as though she wasn't bothered one way or the other whether Philippe took her up on her offer, and, in truth, she wasn't. There were plenty more fish in the sea.

CHAPTER 12

'Hi, it's Philippe.'

'Oh hi. Thanks for calling me back. I wondered if you fancy coming over for dinner tonight?'

'Great idea. There's something I want to run by you anyway and I'd rather ask you in person.' Philippe could sense hesitation on the other end of the phone line. 'Don't panic, it's probably not what you're thinking. I wouldn't be at yours until around eight, if that's okay?'

'Yes. Fine. I thought we could have a takeaway. What do you fancy?'

'Well, apart from you, a curry would go down a treat.'

'Compliment accepted. Anything in particular, or shall I order for both of us?'

'You order and I'll collect, if you text me the address. Shall I get a couple of beers?'

'Okay. See you in a bit.'

Philippe ended the call. He hadn't been looking forward to spending Saturday evening on his own in front of the TV. He had to smile. It was hardly the rock 'n' roll lifestyle most people would associate with a best-selling author. His phone buzzed to alert him to a text message.

That was quick, he thought, glancing at the screen. There was also an alert for a missed call. He didn't recognise the number. It's probably one of those companies telling me how they can help me reclaim mis-sold PPI, he thought, discarding his phone on the console table and taking the stairs two at a time on his way to the bathroom for a quick shower and change of clothes.

Ten minutes later, Philippe, dressed in navy chinos and a light blue jumper, grabbed his car keys and phone and climbed into his Audi A5. He opened Holly's message on his phone and entered the postcode for The Golden Tiger restaurant, in Reading, into his sat-nav before setting off on the hour-long drive.

The traffic on the M4 had been minimal and, having exceeded the speed limit by ten miles an hour all the way, Philippe arrived at The Golden Tiger earlier than anticipated. While he sat on an orange plastic chair waiting for their takeaway to finish cooking, he decided to check the missed call. He was surprised to discover it was from Maddie. He couldn't be sure from the ambiguous nature of the message but did he detect that she was after more than a meal and a movie? He thought about her beautifully sculptured facial features and her lithe, toned body for a moment. There was no denying that she was a stunner and if he wasn't so besotted with Holly he would definitely have been interested in getting to know her better.

The situation with Holly was starting to test his willpower to the limit. He couldn't remember a time since the age of seventeen when he had abstained from sex for more than three months. It was driving him crazy. Maybe, if she said yes to his suggestion of him accompanying her on her next Liberty Sands assignment, she would also agree to let him stay over at her house tonight? He was longing to hold her curvy naked body in his arms again. He had exercised enormous restraint on their cosy nights in but he was not sure how much longer he could keep his sexual urges under control. He had quickly realised that he had been a little premature in giving her the Tiffany engagement ring for Christmas. She hadn't made reference to it at all but at least she hadn't given it back to him. Although his timing had clearly been questionable maybe she hadn't totally dismissed the idea of them ending up together.

Philippe stood up and crossed the few feet to the counter where the brown paper bags containing their dinner and two bottles of Cobra beer were now sitting awaiting collection. He was the only customer in the takeaway section of the restaurant and, as he handed over his credit card to pay, he thought he detected a glimmer of recognition in the eyes of the woman behind the counter. That was one of the problems with his growing fame: his private life was no longer quite so private.

CHAPTER 13

Carol had been very quiet on the bus journey back to Clifton and over their evening meal, and had retired to bed early without her customary mug of warm milk. Helen was still coming to terms with the shocking revelations about Uncle George, as she dried and put away the dishes.

After the regressive episode in the Memorial Garden, the two women had left the park at the opposite end from where they had entered and walked down Green Street. As Helen knew she would, Carol stopped in front of the three-storey terraced house where she had spent her early childhood.

'It's not how I remember it,' she said, rubbing her hands on her temples. 'There was a big wall across the street from our house that I used to bounce my ball against, not houses.'

'That was a long time ago, Carol,' Helen said gently, 'the houses look quite new. Did you live here for very long?'

'Until Daddy died when I was twelve. We were happy here. Mummy didn't have a job; she was a housewife. She was always smiling and singing when she was doing the housework, and she used to come and meet me from school every day, even though it's only three streets away. She was so pretty,' Carol said, a wistful look crossing her face, 'and Daddy used to buy her beautiful clothes and shoes. She had one dress that was my favourite with big purple flowers on a creamy yellow background and a small purple bow underneath the bust line. I think it was Daddy's favourite too. She never wore it again after he died.'

'What happened to your father, Carol?'

'He had a cough,' Carol replied. 'Mummy said it was because he smoked too many cigarettes. When I was very little, I used to sit on his knee when he was smoking. He would purse his lips and puff his cheeks out and then I would clap my hands against them and the smoke would come out in little rings,' she said, smiling at the memory. 'It made me laugh, so we would do it over and over again.' The smile disappeared and in a trembling voice she said, 'But then he got really sick and died. Mummy said it was lung cancer. It broke her heart. She was never the same after that.'

'And what about you? It must have been devastating for you too?'

Carol looked bewildered. 'I couldn't let Mummy see me sad. I had to look after her. She'd lost the person she loved the most in the world. I had to try and help her pain go away.'

Helen watched Carol's face as it contorted with the anguish of remembering the events of almost fifty years previously. 'But you'd lost your dad. She should have been looking after you and reassuring you about how much she loved you. You were only twelve and you needed your mum to be strong for both of you.'

'I knew she loved me,' Carol said, defensively, 'she didn't need to tell me.'

'Okay,' Helen continued, carefully, 'but surely there were other grown-ups around that could help her come to terms with her grief and make her see that she needed to take care of you, not the other way round?'

'Mummy had a brother. When we had to move out of our house, because Mummy couldn't afford the rent, he said we could go and live with him. He was so kind at first. Mummy sometimes had really bad days where she cried continuously and said she had nothing left to live for. Uncle George could see that it upset me and he would give me a hug and tell me she didn't mean it. Then...' her voice faltered, 'then he started to hug me at other times. I didn't like it but I was afraid to tell him to stop in case he threw Mummy and me out. We had nowhere else to go, you see. That's when it started.'

Helen could taste bile rising into her mouth. 'What started, Carol?'

'The night visits,' Carol replied, in a barely audible whisper. 'The first time he came into my room he said it was because he heard me crying. I had been crying, so I believed him. He climbed into my bed and said he would cuddle me until I fell asleep. I didn't push him away. I should have pushed him away,' she said, shaking her head. 'It was all my fault.'

'You mustn't blame yourself,' Helen said, struggling to control her emotions. That bastard had taken advantage of a grieving, frightened child and had somehow made her believe that she was responsible for his disgusting actions. She had an overwhelming desire to put her arms around Carol and tell her that everything was all right but it wasn't, and it never would be, and besides Carol didn't like too much physical contact so would probably push her away. The frail sixty-year old woman standing at her side with her shoulders slumped and looking totally defeated, had been destroyed by a set of circumstances she had no control over. Had the actions of her depraved uncle been the catalyst for her alcohol addiction? Helen wondered.

'You shouldn't have brought me here,' Carol said, belligerently. 'I don't like it. I want to go home,' she said, setting off in the direction of Arkwright Street.

Helen quickly caught up and the two walked to the bus stop in silence. There were so many more questions that she wanted to ask Carol but they would have to wait for now. What was clear to Helen though was that it wasn't only Carol's childhood that had been so brutally cut short. The despicable behaviour of her uncle had impacted her entire life, and the alcohol she had hoped would numb the pain threatened to end it early too.

CHAPTER 14

It was still dark outside when Holly lifted her baby daughter out of the travel crib and laid her on the plastic-coated mat to change her nappy. Rosie had been awake for the past thirty minutes but, instead of crying for attention, she had amused herself with the activity centre attached to the side of her crib. Holly had been woken up by the strains of 'Frère Jacques', which was infinitely preferable to the piercing beeps of her alarm clock. However, after it had played a dozen or more times, a little bit like her hitting the snooze button repeatedly, she decided she had had enough of the melody for one morning. A quick glance at the clock told her it was time to get up anyway if she was going to be ready for the car picking her up at 8 a.m. Already starting to feel the prickle of nerves for her second live appearance on TV, she was grateful for the normality of nappy-changing and getting Rosie dressed for breakfast.

A sliver of electric light was escaping through the small gap under the kitchen door and spilling on to the plush, pearl-grey lounge carpet as Holly carried her baby daughter down the sweeping staircase. She smiled. Robert had been ecstatic when she had asked if he would mind babysitting Rosie for the morning while she went off to the TV studios, now that Harry was back at university for his final term. Not only was he thrilled that Holly was entrusting him with caring for her precious daughter, he had suggested that the two of them stayed over in Woldingham the night before so that she wouldn't need to be up in the middle of the night to get to his before the morning rush hour and gridlock on the M25.

The kettle was boiling merrily as she pushed open the kitchen door. 'Morning, Robert. You didn't need to get up so early, I've got plenty of time to get Rosie's breakfast before I need to get showered.'

'It's nice to have something to get up for,' Robert said, reaching his hands out to relieve Holly of her smiling baby, 'particularly when it's my two favourite girls,' he added, lifting Rosie high above his head and tickling her sides. The little girl responded with delighted giggles.

'Hmmm, I'm not sure that's entirely true. I predict you won't even notice when one of your "favourite" girls has left for work.'

'Of course I will,' Robert said, 'but, I must confess, I am looking forward to a little bit of time on my own with my angel.'

It warmed Holly's heart to see the two of them together. She hadn't wanted to take advantage of Robert's good nature by asking him to look after Rosie but he did seem the obvious choice. He was used to feeding her and changing her and rocking her to sleep, and she had been used to having him in her life since the day she was born.

'So, did I get the right one?' Robert asked, lowering a wriggling Rosie into a high chair and fastening the straps.

Robert had wanted to buy a crib, buggy and high chair to have at his house to make Rosie feel more at home but Holly had insisted that bringing the buggy and the travel crib across in the car wouldn't be a problem. She had also suggested that Rosie could sit in her car seat to eat her meals. Robert didn't think that would be very safe so he had called Harry before he left for Bath and asked him for the make and model of Rosie's high chair and then ordered one online which had been delivered earlier in the week. Although Holly had made noises about Robert spoiling her daughter she was secretly pleased that he was so aware of the importance of familiarity to keep the little girl happy.

'I would be very surprised if you hadn't, seeing as you and Harry were conspiring behind my back. It's so kind of you, Robert, you've thought of everything to try and keep Rosie content,' she said, mixing some apple oatmeal for her daughter. 'Do you want to feed her or should I?'

'I'll do it. I got a little something for you too. It's in the cupboard next to the cooker.'

Holly was intrigued. She opened the cupboard door and there was a bright, shiny stainless steel egg poacher.

'I wasn't sure if you'd be too nervous for a proper breakfast this morning but I got it anyway. I seem to remember the eggs we poached by dropping them into boiling water weren't that successful when we tried them at Christmas.'

Holly had to turn her back on Robert to prevent him seeing a tear form in her eye. She couldn't bear the thought that this special person might spend the rest of his days living alone because he had been so cruelly robbed of the love of his life. 'I think I'll just stick with toast. You're right about the nervous tummy today, but there'll be lots of other opportunities to make use of the poacher, I hope, always assuming Rosie behaves herself, of course. Can I make you some toast too?' she asked, handing over the bowl of baby food.

'Just a cup of tea for me at the moment, thanks. I'll have something a bit later when Rosie's finished her breakfast. I want to give her my full attention, don't I, my angel,' he said, spooning the oatmeal into her obediently open mouth.

Not for the first time Holly felt overwhelmingly sad that Robert and his late wife, Rosemary had never been able to have children. Why must life be so unfair? There were so many unwanted, unloved children in the world who would have been treasured by the Forresters. She herself had fallen pregnant so easily and both occasions were unplanned. It always made her feel guilty, regardless of the depth of love she had for her children.

At 8 a.m. precisely there was a ring on the doorbell. Holly didn't want to make a big fuss over leaving Rosie so she waved to Robert from the top of the stairs and closed the door quietly behind her. It was difficult to suppress a smile when the smartly dressed driver held the door to the back seat of the car open for her and told her to help herself to cold drinks. She had become accustomed to travelling in limousines in her role as undercover travel blogger, Liberty Sands, so the irony of this car also being for Liberty Sands, rather than Holly Wilson, didn't escape her. Maybe I should just change my name and have done with it, she mused. Liberty certainly seemed to have a lot more luck than Holly, even Larry, her agent, had made the contract in the name of Liberty Sands. My agent, she thought, how crazy is that? Apparently, he had made quite a few demands on her behalf, most of which had been rejected for the probationary three-month contract, but he had dug his heels in over the studio sending a car to pick her up and take her home. I could just as easily get the train, she had argued, but Larry was insistent. 'You have to lay the ground rules right at the beginning or people will trample all over you,' he had said. As she sank back into the leather upholstery, Holly was glad that she had been guided by his experience. Not having to rush around on public transport meant that she could read through the notes she had made for this week's appearance in comfort.

Fifty minutes later, with the car in stationary traffic in Streatham and her notes put to one side after she'd read them through half a dozen times, she reached into her bag for her mobile phone. She toyed with it for a few minutes while she tried to decide what she should say to Philippe. He was out of town again for another television interview and Holly frowned, trying to recollect where he said he was going this time. She was pretty sure he had mentioned Dublin but she couldn't remember whether he was doing a breakfast, morning or lunchtime show.

She had had almost a week to think about the suggestion he'd made last Saturday when he'd come to hers for supper and she was still no nearer to a decision. It was just over a year since they had first met in Mauritius and, if he was to be believed, he hadn't slept with another woman in all that time. He had asked if he could accompany her to Mexico on her next assignment, and she was struggling to find a reason to say no. She still fancied him like crazy and, since the day of Rosie's christening when she had voiced her concerns over his drinking habits, he had never had more than one drink in her presence. What's holding me back? she wondered. The fear of getting hurt again or, now that I know him better, the question of whether we've got enough in common to spend the rest of our lives together? One thing they shared was the love of their baby daughter and that was part of Holly's problem. Would he have tried so hard to make a go of things if they didn't have Rosie?

He clearly wanted to stay over last weekend, Holly thought, and, with Harry back at university, there was no reason to deny him, but she did. What is wrong with me? she thought, shaking her head in exasperation. He's handsome, attentive, sexy, successful, and he says he loves me. And I should probably add 'patient' to that, although it seemed his patience was running out. He probably hadn't intended his parting words to sound like an ultimatum, but they had struck a chord with Holly.

'You know I love you,' he had said, 'but I can't wait for ever.'

And he's right, Holly thought, glancing down at the phone in her hand, I'm being selfish by keeping him dangling like this. He deserves a second chance. She tapped in a message:

On the way to show two of *On The Sofa*. Have been thinking about what you said & you're right, am not being fair. Call me after the show xxx

Holly's second appearance on *On The Sofa* had gone much better than her first, at least from her perspective. Annabel had warned her that the director would probably say a few things to her via her earpiece so that she would start getting used to it.

'Just listen to him, but don't reply,' Annabel advised, 'because nobody watching at home will have heard the director speak so, if you answer him, you will sound a little crazy,' she added with a laugh. Simon had been much friendlier with her today too, but it was Richard's comment that had really put a spring in her step.

'Nice one, Holly. You may just have sorted out my summer holiday for me. No need for a debrief today if you want to get off home.'

The only person she hadn't seen that morning was her friend, Maddie. As she passed the make-up room on the way back to her dressing room, she stuck her head round the door.

'I haven't seen Maddie today, Tamsin. Is she not working?'

'She was supposed to be. Richard's furious with her. She had the day off yesterday to go to her sister's wedding in Dublin and she missed her early morning flight back.'

Holly felt like she had been punched in the stomach. She could feel the blood in her veins turn to ice. Maddie had been in Dublin at the same time as Philippe. Coincidence? Holly didn't think so, particularly after Maddie had shown such an interest in him. She stumbled along the corridor to her dressing room, tears blinding her eyes, and slumped down on to the sofa. I guess Philippe simply got tired of waiting for me, she thought, miserably.

CHAPTER 15

Helen walked up the path with a feeling of trepidation. She was starting to feel concerned about Carol, who had remained quiet all week and had gone back to picking at her food. She was also refusing to go for her morning walk, saying she didn't feel well. On Wednesday morning, Helen had come back from the shopping precinct with sugar-coated doughnuts to try and tempt her with a treat, but Carol had said she wasn't hungry and the doughnuts had ended up in the bin. More worryingly, Helen thought she could detect the smell of whisky on her breath. The only bottle in the house was under lock and key in the suitcase in Helen's room. She had checked the bottle with the measurements marked on the side but none was missing, so where had Carol got it from? she wondered.

When Helen had moved in, she had meticulously checked the house from top to bottom for stashes of alcohol. She had even climbed the rickety pull-down ladder into the loft space, despite having serious doubts as to whether the frail Carol would be capable of doing the same thing. It was empty apart from a trunk in the far corner which, on closer inspection, contained old papers and photographs but no bottles. Helen wanted to get to a point in their relationship where Carol would trust her enough to look at the contents of the trunk together, but that was not the priority. The first thing was to stop Carol drinking to excess and that she had succeeded in doing within the first couple of months.

Helen's approach was a bit different. Instead of forcing Carol to go 'cold turkey', she had told her that she must ask every time she wanted a drink. At first Carol would knock back the small measure poured for her and instantly demand another, at which point Helen would remind her that she was only allowed one drink an hour so she would have to wait. Carol's response to this had initially been quite violent but gradually the length of time between drinks got longer until eventually the only drink of the day was at bedtime in hot milk. It would be a devastating blow if all the progress of the past nine months had been lost. Once again, Helen was regretting her decision to take Carol on the trip down memory lane. Maybe it had been too soon but Helen was acutely aware that time was running out for her to get the answer to her burning question, particularly if Carol had started drinking again.

'I'm back,' she called out, closing the front door behind her.

'Hurry up, it's nearly time,' Carol responded, in a voice tinged with excitement.

Relief flooded through Helen. Carol seemed in good spirits. 'I'll just pop these things in the kitchen and put the kettle on. I bought some chocolate brownies today. Would you like one with your coffee?'

'Yes, whatever. You'll miss her if you don't hurry.'

Helen knew that the 'her' in question was Liberty Sands and she was anxious not to miss her appearance too. She wanted to observe Carol's reaction to seeing her again, following her insistence that Liberty Sands was her estranged daughter. Surely it was just the ramblings of someone whose mind was confused by the dementia she suffered from. It was a cruel illness. One moment she would be perfectly lucid and the next she wouldn't even know her own name.

Hastily, Helen poured some milk into a small pan to warm while she put groceries away. She spooned coffee granules into their mugs, put the brownies on a plate, by which time the milk had warmed and the kettle had boiled. She followed Carol's instruction of milk first, topped up with boiling water, to make the perfect milky coffee and was just pushing open the door to the lounge as Annabel introduced the travel segment of *On The Sofa*.

Carol, with her back to the door, appeared to be transfixed. She sat perfectly still listening to every word. There was no sign of the agitation of the previous week. Helen placed the tray on the table and perched on the edge of a chair, making as little noise as possible. Liberty Sands seemed much more assured than she had been on her first show and Helen had to admit that the show's producer had made a very shrewd decision in replacing the ageing Stuart Clapham.

When the segment finished, Carol reached for the remote control to switch off her favourite programme, then turned to face Helen with tears streaming down her cheeks, much to the younger woman's surprise.

'I need you to do something,' she whispered, her words

almost inaudible. 'I need you to write to my daughter and tell her I'm sorry. I'm not a bad person. Really I'm not. The drink made me say and do bad things. I wanted to love her, I-I just couldn't.' Carol seemed to crumple after the effort of her speech.

Helen didn't know what to say. It was pointless suggesting that it was unlikely that Liberty Sands was her estranged daughter. Nothing would be gained by it and it could cause another violent outburst. However faint the possibility was, there would be little harm done in sending a letter to Liberty Sands, care of the television studio. Most likely it would never reach the lady herself but if it did and it turned out that Liberty Sands and Holly Wilson were one and the same person, there may even be a faint hope of them being reunited. Helen's thoughts turned to the trunk in the attic. There would probably be photographs of mother and daughter together and that would add weight to any letter they sent.

'Drink your coffee before it gets cold while I go and fetch some writing paper from my room. We can write the letter and then walk up to the precinct together after lunch and pop it in the post. I don't suppose you've got any photos of Holly as a little girl?' she added casually.

Carol's face brightened. 'Yes, I have. They're up in the loft. What a good idea, Helen. Can you fetch them down?'

'I'll get them right now,' Helen said, excited at the thought of what else she may discover in the trunk which would help fill in some missing pieces of a complicated jigsaw.

CHAPTER 16

All the elation Holly had felt, following her second appearance on *On The Sofa* had evaporated after finding out that Maddie and Philippe had been in Dublin together. Having sent a text message to Philippe on her journey in to work, asking him to call her after the show, the last thing she now wanted to do was speak to him at all. She turned her phone off and stuffed it in her handbag as she climbed into the back of the silver Mercedes.

Mercifully, the car journey back to Woldingham was much quicker than the journey to the studios had been earlier that morning, but it still gave her plenty of time to think about the latest turn of events. As the built-up streets of south London were replaced by the leafy suburbs, Holly decided she had had a lucky escape. She knew she had kept Philippe waiting for a decision about their future for too long but she had wanted to be sure she was doing the right thing for her and their baby. It now seemed she had been wise to take her time. A thought occurred to her. Maybe Maddie wasn't the only fling he'd had. Perhaps she was just the latest conquest in a long string of affairs. Women had been throwing themselves at him since his latest book had been so successful. It was naive of her to think that he had spurned all their advances in favour of cosy nights in with someone who was almost forty and who was keeping him at arm's length.

And then there was the position he had put her in with Maddie. Although she had only known her a couple of weeks they were already becoming good friends. How on earth was she going to face her in a week's time at the studios? How humiliating. Maybe I just won't go back, Holly thought irrationally, as the car pulled into Robert's driveway.

She thanked the driver, unsure whether or not she was supposed to give him a tip, and rang the doorbell. Come on, Robert, she thought impatiently, a sudden overwhelming need to hug her baby daughter enveloping her. The door started to open but it wasn't Robert, it was Nick.

'Holly, you're back early. Robert didn't think you'd be here until at least one o'clock. They're not back from their walk yet. Are you okay? You look upset.'

'I'm fine. I just need to hug Rosie. Which way did they go? I could go and meet them.'

'I'm sorry, I don't know. I was working on some drawings in the office. I'm sure they won't be long though. I'd offer to drive you around the village to look for them but I haven't got the car.'

Looking around, Holly realised that his Range Rover Sport wasn't on the driveway. 'Is it in for a service?' she asked distractedly.

'No. I just fancied a walk. I'm trying to get myself fit again. I've got a big birthday in June, one with a zero on the end.'

'Me too, and I'm suddenly feeling very old.'

'Well, if it makes you feel better, you don't look it. Robert called me through from the office to watch you on TV. You looked amazing, and you sounded so professional. I think Rosie knew it was you too. She stopped building her tower of blocks and stared at the screen.'

Without warning, tears started streaming down Holly's face.

'Hey,' Nick said, 'don't cry. Whatever it is, it can't be that bad. Come on, let's get you inside. I'll make you a cup of tea,' he added, awkwardly putting his arm around her shoulder.

She rested her head against the smooth fabric of his T-shirt for a moment before pushing him away. 'Sorry,' she said, reaching into her handbag for a tissue to wipe her eyes, 'I'm being a drama queen. I was just missing Rosie,' she lied, heading down the staircase, 'we haven't spent much time apart since she was born. You're working; I'll make the tea. Remind me how you take it.'

Five minutes later, each with a warm drink in hand, they sat opposite each other on Robert's beautifully upholstered sofas. Holly was feeling embarrassed about her emotional display and was hiding behind her mug, sipping her chamomile tea.

Nick cleared his throat. 'So, do you want to talk about it?'

Holly lifted her eyes to meet his. They were full of compassion. Or maybe it was pity. In her fragile state, Holly couldn't trust herself to make the distinction between the two. She swallowed hard to prevent the tears starting again. 'Not really.'

'I'm a good listener.'

'Thank you for offering, but it's stuff I need to sort out for myself,' she said, taking another sip of tea.

'I understand. We don't really know each other well enough to be sharing secrets just yet.'

Holly raised her gaze again. Just yet? she thought. What does he mean by that?

As though he had read her mind, Nick said, 'We're probably going to see quite a lot of each other if Robert is going to be your number one babysitter. I come up most days now that I'm working with him. I love it here; the view is so inspiring. Mind you, it's going to get pretty crowded in the office when Harry joins us in June,' he said, before hastily adding, 'in a nice way of course.'

'Harry's looking forward to it. He can't quite believe his luck. Not only has he got Robert as his mentor and the Philmore refurbishment to cut his teeth on, he's got you working alongside him if he needs advice. I thought he wasn't starting until July though? We were planning on going away somewhere for a joint celebration of me starting a new decade and him finishing uni.'

'I just assumed he would want to get started straight away, I'm sure he won't want me stealing the limelight for any of his creative ideas in LA. Where were you thinking of going?'

'I'm not sure. In some respects it's a bit of a busman's holiday for me, except that Harry and I won't be staying in a five-star hotel.'

'What about Mauritius? The sale on Sunset Cottage should be completed by then. I'm sure Robert would be more than happy to have you stay.'

'I don't think so, Nick. Mauritius is somewhere I would rather forget. Too many unhappy memories for me I'm afraid.'

'Ah, you mean Rosemary. You know, I must confess I was surprised that Robert went ahead with the purchase but we all have different ways of dealing with life's tragedies, I guess.'

And I don't seem to deal with them very well, Holly thought. 'It's not just Rosemary. There are times when I wish that I'd never set foot on Mauritius.'

'But then you wouldn't have met Robert, and Harry wouldn't have an amazing career to look forward to. Not to mention falling in love with Philippe and having your beautiful baby. You have a lot to thank Mauritius for.'

Holly studied Nick. Was he fishing for a clue as to why she had broken down in tears earlier? Until she had decided how she was going to handle the situation with Philippe, the last thing she needed was anyone else's opinion.

'You're right. I shouldn't be so ungrateful. If it wasn't for Mauritius, I wouldn't have Robert or my darling Rosie.'

She took another sip of her chamomile tea. I need to change the subject, she thought.

'So, tell me a bit more about yourself. All I really know, apart from you being an architect, is that, like me, you're from Nottingham and you have the same big birthday as me coming up in June. What date is yours?'

'The nineteenth of June.'

'Are you serious? That's the same day as me.'

'Really? What are the chances of that?'

'How are you planning on celebrating?'

'Probably just with the twins.'

'Oh right. Robert mentioned you're separated from their mother.'

'Divorced now. The decree absolute came through last month.'

'Are you happy about that?'

'Very. We should have split up years ago but we stayed together for the sake of the twins.'

'I didn't realise people still did that. Everything seems so throwaway these days. At the first sign of trouble, couples who a few years before swore undying love for each other just throw the towel in. There seems to be this feeling that the grass is always greener elsewhere.'

'Well, we gave it our best shot, but the bottom line is that we got married for the wrong reason. We were young and in love and then Caroline fell pregnant. Marriage seemed the right thing to do but really we were little more than kids ourselves. It was a massive learning curve having twins and I don't think our relationship ever recovered from not having enough time for each other.'

'You don't regret having them though?'

'No. They are absolutely the best thing that has happened in my life so far. Some men don't really get involved in the everyday bits of raising their children, they just like the "kicking a ball around" and "going for a pizza" bits, but I was a proper hands-on dad from the start. Caroline suffered terribly with the baby blues. She wouldn't even hold them for the first couple of weeks, despite the best efforts of the midwife. I don't know if she ever really bonded with them properly.'

'That's so sad. I can't imagine a mother not experiencing

the all-consuming love I felt for Harry. I never wanted to put him down but I suppose it was different because there was only me most of the time. Don't laugh, but I used to get jealous of the health visitor if she held him for just a little too long.'

'That doesn't surprise me. I remember the look on your face the first time we met, when you came out of the kitchen to see me cuddling Rosie. It was terrifying.'

'I am a bit over-protective,' Holly admitted, 'but maybe that's because she was premature and I could so easily have lost her.'

'I was teasing,' Nick said.

'Oh. Sorry. I seem to be having a sense of humour bypass today. I promise I'm not always like this, bursting into tears in front of someone I barely know.'

'Don't apologise. It must be tough bringing up a baby on your own and trying to get to grips with a new career. You shouldn't be so hard on yourself. Apparently, my real mother couldn't cope with me even though she had the support of a loving husband.'

'What do you mean?'

'I was given up for adoption when I was a month old. I was a twin too. Maybe it runs in my genes. As far as I understand my real mother was on the verge of a nervous breakdown trying to look after both babies. It seems she was neglecting me in preference for my twin so I was removed from her care. Not the greatest of starts in life,' Nick said, smiling ruefully.

'That's so awful. I remember in the film *Sophie's Choice* when the mother had to decide which child she was going to keep. I was hysterical just watching it. I can't imagine what it must be like to live with a choice like that. I wonder if she ever forgave herself?'

'I don't know and I've never had the desire to find out. It's been challenging enough trying to hide what was going on between Caroline and me from our boys without complicating things further.'

'But what about your twin? Didn't you want to try and reconnect with them? I thought twins had a special relationship?'

'You hear stories about twins who were separated at birth feeling incomplete and bereft without their other half, but I've never experienced that. I hadn't felt the need to try and trace them, partly because I'm not even sure they know I exist, but with our fortieth birthday coming up I did give it a bit of thought.'

'And?'

'And I decided against it. This divorce from Caroline feels like an opportunity to start afresh, a chance to rid myself of negativity in my life. The last thing I want is to discover that my twin has had as messed up a life as me. I'd rather hang on to the belief that they had a happier childhood than I did.'

Holly was watching Nick closely over the rim of her china mug. There was a sadness in his beautiful light green eyes that she hadn't noticed before, but not a hint of jealousy or resentment towards his unknown sibling. Holly knew from personal experience what it was like to have an unhappy childhood. 'I'm sorry things didn't work out with your adoptive parents,' she said.

'It wasn't really their fault. They'd been trying for a baby of their own for ten years without success when they adopted me. Within a year of taking me on, my adoptive mother fell pregnant and then went on to have three more children. I always felt like the cuckoo in the nest. Maybe that's why the relationship with Caroline got so serious so quickly. It felt good to have someone care for me.'

'How on earth have you turned out to be such a nice human being after all you've been through?'

'How do you know I'm nice?' Nick said, a twinkle returning to his eyes. 'As you said earlier, we barely know each other.'

'Well, I feel like I know you a lot better now and I like what I've seen so far.'

A slow flush of embarrassment crept up Nick's cheeks.

'I'm so pleased I've found someone else that happens to. Maybe it's a Nottingham thing,' Holly said, laughing.

CHAPTER 17

'What are you doing up there?' Carol called from the foot of the precarious loft ladder.

Helen, bent almost double in the shallow loft space, replied, 'I won't be a minute.'

The trunk had been heavier than she had anticipated and had proved impossible to move on her own, so her plan to drag it to the loft hatch and hand things down to Carol had to be revised. After repeatedly crawling across the cramped area, with bundles of papers and photograph albums tucked under her free arm, Helen was covered in dust and sweating profusely but at least the entire contents of the trunk were now in piles within easy reach of the top of the ladder. She carefully stepped backwards on to the top rung and descended to halfway before picking up the first pile and then continuing her descent to the landing.

'Phew. Not as easy as I thought it was going to be. Do you want to take these downstairs to the lounge or shall we put everything on the bed in the spare room and take things down one at a time?'

Carol was grinning. 'You've got a big black smudge

above your top lip. It looks like a moustache.'

'I'm glad you're finding this so entertaining,' Helen said. 'Bedroom or lounge?'

'Lounge, I think, then we'll have everything close to hand rather than going up and down stairs.'

'Can you manage to take this pile down while I get the next lot?'

'I'm not helpless you know,' Carol said, taking the papers out of Helen's arms.

Helen shuddered, remembering the night a few weeks ago when Carol had fallen headlong down the stairs. For one terrible moment, as she had stood looking down on the crumpled body, Helen had feared that Carol might be dead. As she had rushed to Carol's side, she had silently pleaded, don't let her die before I have a chance to tell her. The relief that had flooded through her when Carol had moaned in pain was immeasurable.

'Well be careful,' Helen said over her shoulder, as she started back up the ladder. She re-emerged moments later with half a dozen photo albums and put them at the top of the stairs for Carol's next trip before heading back up the ladder. When she came back down, Carol was sat on the top step, a plaid photo album open on her lap.

'Look, Helen. I told you Mummy was pretty. This was taken on her honeymoon in Scarborough. I think Daddy must have been taking the picture.'

'It looks cold,' Helen said, peering over the older woman's shoulder and noticing the choppy waves and the strands of hair that had escaped from the neat hairstyle and were blowing across the woman's face. 'What month were they married?'

'It must have been March. Mummy said I was conceived

on their honeymoon and my birthday is Boxing Day.'

'So you're a Christmas Carol.'

'Yes. Not very original is it. Daddy wanted to call me Beverley but Mummy over-ruled him. I think I prefer Carol.' She snapped the album shut. 'These aren't the right ones. These are older pictures. We need to find the ones with Holly in them.'

'Yes we do. You take those down and I'll get the next lot. Once we've got everything in the lounge we can start to look properly,' she said. Who knows what we may find, she thought, with a tingle of excitement.

By the time all the boxes, albums and loose papers were neatly piled on the floor next to the television in the lounge it was time for lunch. Both women were keen to get on with their search so a cheese and pickle sandwich was decided on as a quick bite. The unwashed plates were left on the drainer, which was most unusual for house-proud Helen.

'Any ideas which album the pictures of Holly will be in?' Helen asked. 'What about this one? It looks very 1970s.'

The album Helen was holding had big purple and orange flowers on it.

'You're about a decade out. That's much more 1960s. Very Mary Quant and flower power. I had a minidress with a pattern similar to that. It's worth having a look, though; I can't remember what's in any of them. I haven't set eyes on them since Holly left. I made her dad put them in the loft. I couldn't bear to look at her after what she did.'

Helen noticed an edge creeping into Carol's voice. The last thing she wanted was for Carol to change her mind about searching through the pictures for a suitable one of her daughter. It was also important to try and keep her calm if she was going to try and squeeze information out of her.

'Let's look together,' she said, moving next to her on the sofa. 'You can tell me who everyone is.'

Carol was more animated than Helen had ever seen her. The purple and orange album was filled with photographs of family holidays when Carol was very young. Most Nottingham families who went on an annual seaside holiday headed towards the east coast, due to its proximity; Skegness and Mablethorpe were particular favourites, along with Great Yarmouth. However, Carol's Aunty Ethel owned a guest house in Blackpool, so that was where the Atkinson family headed each August. There was a picture of Carol and her mum climbing aboard a tram and another of them sitting in deckchairs on the not-so golden sands, eating their sandwiches. There was one of Carol sitting astride a donkey, waving excitedly towards the camera and another with her dad in a small rowing boat on the boating lake.

Two things were constant in all the photographs, Helen noticed. Carol had the bright-eyed smile of innocence and her father had a cigarette in his hand. Knowing that the latter had unwittingly caused the extinction of the former, saddened Helen.

The last picture in the album made Carol laugh. 'I took this one,' she said, pointing to a photograph of her parents from the neck down. 'Daddy said I must have tilted the camera when I pressed the button. He still put it in the album because it was my first attempt and he didn't want to discourage me from trying again. I didn't get another chance. He was too poorly to go on holiday the following year. Now I come to think of it, that was the last time I ever went to Blackpool.'

'Would you like to go back and see all the old places you used to visit? Maybe I could organise a trip for us?'

Carol shook her head. 'It wouldn't be the same. It would just cloud the memories I have. You do understand don't you?'

'Of course. And you're right,' she added, remembering how she had desperately clung on to happy memories of her married life, banishing all thoughts of her husband's second family. She picked up a dark green album edged with gold. 'Shall we try this one next?'

On the first page there were four photographs. Carol had transformed from a smiling ten-year-old to a smiling eighteen-year-old, but the smile no longer reached her eyes. She was wearing a cream-coloured mididress and was holding a bunch of pale pink peonies, and her arm was linked through that of a dashingly handsome man, who looked several years older than her. They were standing at the top of a short flight of steps in front of a red-brick building, and paper petals were raining down on them. It was Carol's wedding day.

Helen watched Carol carefully. She was staring at the page, almost trance-like.

'I'd always dreamed of getting married in a church,' she said eventually, in a voice little more than a whisper. 'I was going to wear a long white dress with a flowing train and a fine lace veil covering my face, held in place by a sparkly tiara. My bridesmaids were going to be dressed in pink and I'd always pictured Daddy in a grey suit with a pink buttonhole when we walked down the aisle together, before he gave me away to the love of my life.' She stopped, a puzzled look on her face. 'Daddy didn't even come to the wedding. I think he must have been too ashamed of me.'

A lump of pity rose in Helen's throat. 'He wanted to be there, Carol,' she said gently, 'but he couldn't. He would have been very proud of you. You looked so beautiful.'

'He would not,' Carol spat, rounding on Helen. 'You don't know anything. He was ashamed. He knew what I'd done. They don't let bad people get married in church, you know, at least they didn't in those days. We had to settle for a Registry Office and Mummy told me I couldn't wear white because I wasn't a virgin. She said I was lucky that William was taking me on. She said most people wouldn't give me a second chance; I was damaged goods. William didn't care. He just wanted to marry me. The saddest thing is that he worshipped the ground I walked on and I don't know if I ever really loved him. I was just so grateful that he was taking me away from the hell I'd been living through, to start a new life. You see, Helen, I'm a truly horrible person. Not content with wrecking my own life, I had to ruin his as well. He must have realised I didn't love him soon after Holly was born. I couldn't bear him touching me. I made so many excuses to keep him away: I was breast-feeding or I was tired because Holly wasn't sleeping, and I must have claimed a hundred headaches. When I felt really guilty about denying him I used to drink so that I could blot it all out.'

So that must have been the start of her drink problem, Helen thought. How desperately sad that she didn't seek professional help, although at the time, it wasn't the done thing. To Helen, it sounded like an obvious case of post-natal depression.

'I can't blame him for lavishing all his love on Holly,' Carol continued, 'at least she loved him back. I couldn't bear the thought of having any more children. I couldn't go through it again,' she said. Then in a whisper: 'What if they'd taken that one as well?'

Helen gripped the arm of the sofa. This was it. This was when Carol would tell her about the baby that had been taken away from her. She waited, barely able to breathe, but Carol seemed exhausted after her outburst and remained silent.

Although Helen was desperate to keep her talking she could sense that the moment had passed. She would have to be patient. 'Well, I don't know about you, but I could murder a cup of tea. Let's have a break from the photographs and sit out in the sun while it's still warm.'

Carol seemed to rally. 'No. I want to find the pictures of Holly,' she replied, turning to the next page in the album. 'You put the kettle on while I keep looking. We've still got the letter to write and I want to get this in the post today.'

Carol didn't raise her eyes from the album as Helen went into the kitchen, her mind racing after what she had just heard. Carol had been so close to talking about the other baby, the one Helen was there to find out about. She barely had time to flip the top of the kettle open and place it under the running tap before a shout from the lounge had her hurrying back through.

'What is it, Carol? What did you find?'

'You see,' she said, a triumphant look on her face, 'I told you that Liberty person is really my Holly.'

Carol had started on a new album and was only a couple of pages in. She was jabbing her finger at a picture that did look remarkably like a younger version of Liberty Sands off the television. Helen leaned in for a closer inspection. The girl in the photo looked to be in her late teens and was the image of her father in the wedding photos that Helen had seen only a few minutes before. Her dark curly hair was tied up in a ponytail and she was wearing denim shorts and a red-and-white striped T-shirt.

'Was this taken in your garden?'

'Yes. She was always out there helping her dad. She probably only did it to keep out of my way. I wasn't very nice to her most of the time,' Carol confessed. 'I wanted to be, but then she would say something or do something to annoy me and I would get angry.'

The alcohol hadn't helped Carol cope with her child, Helen realised. 'Is that a bunch of sweet peas she's holding?'

'Probably,' she said peering closely at the photo. 'They were Will's favourites. He used to grow them every year. I've never been able to stand the sickly sweet smell of them since he died.'

'How old is Holly in that photo?'

'It would have been around her nineteenth birthday. She'd just come home from her first year at Bath university. We were both really proud of her, although I never managed to tell her as much. Neither her dad nor I had gone to university, you see. It's hard to believe I was already married at the age she was there.'

'Are there any other photos taken around that time? Maybe one with her hair down?'

Carol turned to the next page. It was empty, as were the remaining pages of the album.

'It looks like that must have been the last one we took of her,' Carol said, slightly bemused. 'I'd forgotten how skinny she was when she came home. She doesn't look pregnant does she?'

'Pregnant?' The word was out of Helen's mouth before she could stop herself.

'I thought you knew. I'm sure I told you that was why she ran away from home. She wanted to keep the baby but she refused to tell us who the father was. I got my own back on her, though,' she said, malice creeping into her voice, 'I told him she was dead when he came looking for her.'

'When who came looking for her?' Helen asked, a chill creeping into her bones.

'The baby's father. It was a boy. I only saw it once, at Will's funeral.' Carol winced at the painful memory. 'I wish I could have kept the boy, he would have been a lot less trouble, but Will thought I should keep the girl after what happened with the first one.'

Helen was confused. Clearly Carol's alcohol-damaged brain was jumbling things up and she was making no sense.

'We'd better make a start on the letter now that we've found a picture,' Carol said. 'If we hurry you can still get it in today's post.'

CHAPTER 18

The sound of the seagulls soaring overhead in the leaden grey sky and the taste of salt in the air was a salve for Holly's aching heart as she climbed out of her car and stretched her legs. This had turned into a very long day. On the drive back to her little terraced house earlier that afternoon she had reached a decision. She suspected that Philippe might come looking for her if she continued to refuse to take his calls and she wasn't yet ready to confront him about his and Maddie's trip to Dublin. She needed to get away for a few days to clear her head. It wouldn't be fair to land on Harry's doorstep with Rosie in tow when he and his flatmates were in the final stages of exam revision and dissertation writing for their finals. Although she adored Robert, he was Philippe's friend too and would have divided loyalties, besides it would be the first place he would come looking if he wanted to find her. There was only one other person she felt she could call at such short notice.

Fortunately, Rosie's travel cot and pushchair were already in the car but, even though it had taken her less than thirty minutes to pack a bag for the two of them, they had still hit heavy traffic on the M4 heading west, after their short detour via the post office. The Friday afternoon exodus from London had started earlier than she had expected and it had taken three hours to reach the outskirts of Swansea. Rosie, who had slept for most of the journey after tiring herself out at Robert's house, was awake and fractious. She's probably hungry or thirsty or both, Holly thought as she undid the straps of the baby seat and lifted her baby daughter out of the car, and she definitely needs her nappy-changing, she realised as a faintly unpleasant aroma hit her nostrils. Holly swung the baby bag up on to her shoulder and crossed the tarmac driveway to where Gareth was standing in the open doorway, framed by the glow of the hall light beyond.

'Crikey, she's grown a lot since Christmas. What on earth have you been feeding her?'

Holly blushed. 'Mostly me,' she admitted, 'although she's on formula now that she has a couple of teeth and she's has been having solid food as well for the last couple of months. Thanks for letting us come and stay with you for a few days. I really appreciate it.'

'How could I refuse my two favourite girls?'

'I heard that,' came Megan's voice, from somewhere beyond Gareth's solid frame.

'Now I'm in trouble,' Gareth whispered, winking at Holly.

Holly responded with a weak smile. She was emotionally and physically drained. All she really wanted to do was to curl up into a tight ball and go to sleep but now it appeared she would have to be sociable this evening.

As though he had read her mind, Gareth said, 'Megan's

not stopping. She dropped by to help me make up your bedroom and then offered to put a casserole in the oven for our dinner. She's a good sort is Megan.'

'Yes, she is,' Holly said, feeling guilty for her ungracious thoughts. 'I hope you tell her how much you appreciate everything she does for you.'

'I don't need to. She knows.'

'I'd better get the rest of the things in from my car before it gets dark. Do you think Megan would mind holding Rosie for a minute for me?'

'Don't you trust me to hold her, Holly?'

The pause was just a fraction too long before Holly answered, 'Of course, if you can manage her wriggling around, I just didn't want you to lose your balance. She's been sat in her car seat for the best part of five hours today. She probably can't wait for me to put her blanket down so that she can have a bit of a crawl around. She's so funny; she pulls her knees up under her tummy and then tries to move her arms forwards. Most of the time she ends up going backwards. Here you go,' Holly said, handing Rosie over into his outstretched arms.

'She's starting to look like you now she's got a bit of hair. You're going to be a beauty, little Rosie, just like your mummy,' Gareth said to the baby, but the last part of his sentence was lost to Holly as she was already halfway back across the tarmac towards the car.

Five minutes later, all the paraphernalia that was required when travelling with a young baby was piled up in Gareth's hallway.

'Right, young lady,' Holly said, retrieving Rosie from Gareth's lap, 'we'd better go and change your nappy.'

'I'll help you take your stuff up to the spare bedroom

before I go,' Megan offered. 'Have you got any bottles of formula made up that you want warming while you're changing her bottom?'

'Thanks, Megan. It seems like you're familiar with young babies,' Holly said, handing her a chunky baby bottle.

'I should be,' she said, taking the bottle and putting it in an empty jug, which she then filled to halfway with water from the freshly boiled kettle. 'I'm the eldest of seven children spread out over twenty years. I've done my fair share of feeding and winding and changing nappies. It's no wonder I don't want any of my own,' she said, leading the way up the staircase with its handrails on both sides to assist Gareth.

Holly couldn't help thinking that was a shame. Megan had all the attributes to make a good mother. She was calm, patient, kind and always smiling. 'You never know,' Holly said, 'you might change your mind when you find your Mr Right.'

'Maybe I already have, and maybe he doesn't want children either.'

Doesn't want or can't have? Holly wondered. It was obvious to Holly that Megan believed Gareth to be her Mr Right. She wondered if the accident twenty years earlier had left him incapable of fathering children. Perhaps that was why Megan had voiced her lack of desire to have babies within earshot of Gareth: she wanted him to know that not having children was not an issue for her.

'Does he know how you feel about him?' Holly said, gently lying Rosie down on the changing mat that Megan had placed on the freshly made-up bed.

'Who?'

'Gareth.'

'It doesn't matter how I feel. He's happy to have me around as a friend and I'd rather have that than nothing. He'll always be in love with you so he doesn't look at anyone else in that way.'

'Really? We were together such a long time ago, Megan, and for most of the time we were apart, he thought I was dead. I can't believe he still has feelings for me.'

'He has always referred to you as the love of his life, even when he thought you were dead. He's always been very clear that no one could ever take your place. He was really excited when you rang out of the blue to say that you were coming to visit.'

Holly felt a pang of guilt.

'Please don't hurt him, Holly. He's suffered so much and things are finally starting to go well for him. Harry coming into his life, and patching things up with his mum and dad; these things have made him even more determined to work hard on his physiotherapy exercises so that he'll be more mobile again. He's even been seeing a therapist to try and sort out his anger management issues. The last thing any of us wants is a setback.'

Holly deftly fastened the tags of the clean nappy at Rosie's waist, and popped her feet back inside the stretchy velour sleepsuit. 'How old are you, Megan?'

'Twenty-eight.'

'Well, you have a very mature head on your shoulders. Do you want me to tell him how you feel about him?'

Megan looked mortified. 'No. It would ruin everything. I couldn't bear it if things felt awkward between us. Don't you have any feelings for him any more?'

'Of course I have feelings for him. He was my first love

97

and he'll always have a special place in my heart. But I've spent twenty years loving the Gareth I knew back then and he's not the same person now. Nor am I for that matter,' Holly said, lifting Rosie off the mat and sitting her on her hip.

'Are you girls all right up there?' Gareth called from the foot of the staircase.

'Just coming,' they chorused.

'Promise me you won't say anything,' Megan pleaded.

'It's really none of my business. It's for you and Gareth to sort out.' And besides, Holly thought, I've got enough problems with my own love life without interfering with anyone else's.

CHAPTER 19

'I can't believe she's doing this again,' Philippe railed, slumping down on the red Chesterfield sofa in the corner of Jo's office. 'She asked me to ring her after her show on Friday. I was doing a lunchtime show in Dublin that didn't finish until two in the afternoon, then when I rang, her phone went straight to voicemail and it's been doing it over the whole weekend. Surely she can't be that mad at me because I was a couple of hours late ringing her?'

Jo yawned, feigning disinterest. 'Did you try her home number?'

'Of course, I'm not stupid. That went straight to voicemail too. Yesterday afternoon I even drove to her house in Reading.'

Jo raised her eyebrows.

'I was worried about her,' Philippe said, defensively. 'I thought maybe she was ill and couldn't get to the phone or something. There was no reply when I knocked, and I had a good look around and couldn't see her car.'

'What about the architect chap you're both friendly with? Maybe she went to stay with him for a few days?'

'Robert, you mean. Well, she did tell me she was staying at his on Thursday night because he was babysitting Rosie on Friday morning but, according to him, she left straight after lunch. Why is she doing this, Jo? I really thought she was ready to give us another chance. Instead, she does a bloody disappearing act.'

Jo kept her head down, examining the papers on her desk, so Philippe couldn't see the look of satisfaction on her face. 'Have you ever considered that maybe you and Holly are just not suited?'

'I don't even know why I'm talking to you about it. I might have known you'd say that. Holly and I are made for each other. I fell in love with her the moment I laid eyes on her and I'm pretty sure she felt the same way. She is the *only* woman I have ever felt this way about.'

The emphasis on the word 'only' cut Jo to the quick, underlining that she, like all his other conquests, had been nothing more than a fling.

'I'm barely drinking, I'm ignoring advances from other women and I'm even putting up with only seeing my little girl when Holly invites me over. It's breaking my heart. I want to be there to see Rosie's first step and hear her speak her first word.'

'Are you sure it's Holly you're in love with and not your baby daughter?'

'Aren't you bloody listening to me, Jo? You seem to forget that I was desperate to find Holly before I knew she was pregnant with our baby.' He paused. 'You don't think that's what is holding Holly back from committing to me, do you? Maybe she thinks Rosie is my priority too? I don't know what more I can do to show her how serious I am about her,' he added, resignation creeping into his voice.

It was the use of the word 'more' that captured Jo's attention. What had he already done? 'Well, taking her out for an occasional dinner and going round to hers to watch a movie isn't really much of an indication of your commitment to her long term. Women want something more… tangible,' she said, hoping Philippe wouldn't realise she was digging.

'You mean like a Tiffany diamond engagement ring?'

Jo gulped. 'Ah, yes. That would be enough for most women.'

'You forget: Holly's not most women. Why does she have to be so bloody stubborn?'

Jo's pulse was racing. Had he actually proposed to Holly and she had turned him down? Jo had to know. 'So…' she said, as casually as she could, 'you've actually popped the question?'

'Not exactly. I gave her a ring at Christmas. I've never seen her wear it but she didn't give it back either so maybe she's thinking it over. Perhaps I was rushing her.'

'That was four months ago. Haven't you mentioned it since?' Jo asked, incredulous.

'I guess I hoped she would turn up wearing it on one of our dates.'

'For someone who writes so believably as a woman, you really don't understand us very well. What you thought was a romantic proposal, she probably thought was a cowardly cop out. No wonder you haven't seen her wearing it, she's most likely flogged it to pay a few bills.'

'And why would she need to do that?' Philippe demanded. 'Maybe because you're so jealous of her you won't give her any work? Well, she doesn't need the crumbs you throw her way. Now she's on television, she's probably earning more than you!'

There was a tap on the door and Alice's apologetic face appeared.

'Um, sorry to interrupt, but the post room just delivered this for Philippe,' she said, extending a small padded envelope in his direction. 'It says "personal" so I didn't want to open it, unless you want me to, of course.'

Philippe took the package in his hand and stared down at it. He recognised the handwriting and felt the outline of a small rectangular box through the padding. He didn't need to open it; he knew what was inside. He thrust it in his jacket pocket.

'You'd better cancel any public appearances for the next couple of weeks. No, make that the next couple of months. I need to get away. I've got a book to write,' he said, pushing past Alice in his rush to leave Jo's office.

CHAPTER 20

'You have no idea how much better I feel after spending the past few days with you,' Holly said, smiling gratefully at Gareth. 'No wonder you chose to come and live here. It's magical. I love the wide-open spaces and the feeling that every breath is a lungful of fresh air. I want to bottle it and take it home with me.'

'I don't know about bottling the fresh air, but you could certainly take some of the rain back with you. Are you sure that plastic is waterproof? We don't want Rosie getting wet.'

Holly smiled. 'Don't fuss. Robert bought the buggy for Rosie so it's top of the range. She's probably warmer in there than most people are in their houses.'

The two of them were walking along the promenade in Mumbles, both wrapped up in hooded jackets to protect them from the biting wind blowing in off the sea and the sideways driving rain it had brought with it. Gareth was pushing the buggy, leaning on it slightly for a bit of support and balance. To the casual observer, they probably looked like a couple who had decided to start their family in later life. The irony was not lost on Holly.

She had dreamed of moments like this for many years.

There was no denying that she and Gareth had a special connection. Over the past five days they had never been apart, except at bedtime. They were totally relaxed in each other's company; preparing food, eating food, playing with Rosie and walking Gareth's golden retriever, Ben. It was the closest thing to normal family life that Holly had ever experienced. The conversation had never felt forced and when there was silence it was companionable, not awkward. Gareth hadn't quizzed her about her reasons for the impromptu visit and she hadn't offered any explanation. She had simply been happy. She felt almost resentful at the thought of having to go back to London the following day for the next *On The Sofa*.

There had been plenty of time while she was lying alone in bed in Gareth's spare room to consider how she was going to behave around Maddie. She had reached the conclusion that it would be best to pretend she didn't know that the two of them had been in Dublin at the same time unless Maddie mentioned it, in which case she would reveal that she and Philippe were no longer seeing each other. That way there would be no awkwardness working together, although Holly couldn't imagine how they could possibly remain friends. As for Philippe, her plan was to speak with him before her forthcoming trip to Mexico to try and reach an amicable arrangement regarding access to Rosie.

'A penny for them,' Gareth said, interrupting her thoughts.

'Oh, I was just thinking how happy and relaxed I feel right at this moment and how it all has to end tomorrow.'

'Does it? If you love it so much here, you could always

up sticks and move. There's nothing much keeping you in Reading, is there? I mean, it's not as though you're from there, is it? You don't even work there, and it would only be a bit further for Harry to drive from Bath. It doesn't really matter where you're based for your copy-editing work and you could fly to your exotic locations from Cardiff.'

'There are a couple of flaws in your plan,' Holly said, smiling. 'Harry finishes at Bath in a couple of months and then he'll be based in Surrey, miles away from here. And you're forgetting about my new job for *On The Sofa*. It's bad enough getting into London from Reading. It would mean a night away from home every week and who would have Rosie for me? Robert has been fantastic since she was born, and it would break his heart if he didn't get to see so much of her. It's gone part of the way to filling the massive void in his life that Rosemary left.'

'There's nothing keeping him in Surrey now though is there. With what he'd get for his amazing house he could buy a huge mansion here in Wales with spectacular views of the sea.'

'Actually, I think he has an altogether different kind of sea view in mind. He's in the process of buying a place in Mauritius. I guess if he moves out there permanently he won't be able to see much of Rosie anyway.'

'So you're warming to the idea then?'

Holly laughed. 'Are you working for the Welsh Tourist Board or something?'

'I've just enjoyed having you around. I'd forgotten how good for me you are.'

Holly didn't know what to say, so she said nothing.

'By the way, I forgot to mention that Mum and

Dad have sold their place in LA. They're going to get a condominium on the beach in Malibu, so they can go back for holidays, but they're coming back to live in Wales. I've been doing a property search for them so just let me know if you want me to look for you too,' he said with a twinkle in his eye.

'You're very persistent,' Holly replied, 'but I wouldn't want to tread on Megan's toes.'

'What's Megan got to do with anything? Sure, she's a nice enough girl with a heart of gold, but she's way too young for me. She's got her whole life ahead of her. Why would she want to be saddled with an old crock like me?'

'Maybe you should ask her. Age is just a number, and has nothing to do with feelings. I sense that she might have a bit of a soft spot for you,' Holly said, careful not to give anything away after promising Megan that she wouldn't.

'You're wrong. Megan and I are friends, good friends, but you and I are soul mates. Once you've realised that flighty French writer isn't the one for you, just remember that I'll still be here, waiting.'

Gareth had stopped walking and was looking down at Holly. She had forgotten the intensity of his beautiful green eyes that now exhibited a flicker of hope. Had it been thoughtless of her to come running to him because she feared Philippe had been unfaithful?

'I mean it, Holly. You and I were destined to be together. Much as I adored Kate, I only asked her to marry me because I was so grateful to her for rescuing me from the abyss of hopelessness after my accident.' There was a tremble of emotion in Gareth's voice. He paused, looking out to sea, as though trying to regain his composure.

Holly could barely breathe. For the first time since they had been reunited, Gareth was talking calmly about his life-altering experience in America. Obviously the therapy sessions Megan had mentioned were having a positive effect, but Holly could still remember the aggressive way he had reacted when she had tried to broach the subject last summer. He had scared her with his sudden mood swing that night and she couldn't allow herself to forget it. No matter how much of her life she had spent loving him nothing would ever be the same between them in the future.

Gareth turned back to her. 'If she had lived and we had got married it probably wouldn't have worked out because she never knew the real me. She looked after me and I loved her for it but I never felt for her in the same way I feel for you. The shock of losing her unlocked something in my head and I started to remember you, to remember us. I love you, Holly. I always have and I always will.'

The rain was streaming down Holly's upturned face, disguising the tears that were now mingling with it. There was a time when Holly's heart would have done a double somersault on hearing those words from Gareth, but that time was gone. True, she felt happy and content in his company but surely she was entitled to want more than that from a relationship? She was still young enough to want love and passion. His face was moving towards hers. She couldn't allow him to kiss her; it just wouldn't be fair. She turned her head and his lips landed on her damp cheek.

'I can't, Gareth,' she said, pulling away from him.

'I'm sorry. I didn't mean to do that, but you look so

beautiful standing there in the rain. There's no rush. I can wait for ever if that's how long it takes for you to love me again.'

Holly's heart was aching. At that moment she fervently wished she had never set eyes on Philippe, then none of this would have happened and she could have clung on to loving the memory of Gareth. She had assured Megan that she wouldn't hurt him but neither did she want to give him false hope.

'Gareth, I don't want you to wait for me. I've spent half my life clinging on to the memory of loving who we were and what we had, but neither of us are the same people. I've loved spending time with you these past few days; apart from my children and Robert, you are the closest thing to family I have, but it has made me realise that my feelings for you are different now. Please don't waste your time hoping that I'll change my mind because I won't. I love you like the brother I never had and for me it will never be any more than that. I hope you understand, Gareth, and that we can still have our special relationship?'

Gareth said nothing for a few moments. He turned his head towards the murky grey-brown of the distant horizon, the rain pelting him full in the face.

'You'll always be the most special person in my life,' he said, the words swept away on the wind, as soon as he had spoken them.

'I'm sorry, I missed that. What did you say?'

He turned back to face her, his face a mask of calm. 'I said, of course we'll always have a special relationship.'

Holly breathed a sigh of relief. She couldn't bear the thought of losing him from her life having waited so long to find him. 'Promise me one thing,' she said.

'Try me.'

'Please give some thought to what I said about Megan. You're her world, Gareth. If you let her in to yours I think you two could be very happy together.'

Before Gareth could answer, Rosie started to cry.

'She's hungry,' Holly said, glad of the interruption. 'Shall we head back to yours or do you think that café may be able to warm Rosie's bottle?' she asked, indicating a large glass structure at the end of the promenade.

From her vantage point inside Verdi's some two hundred yards away, Megan watched as Holly pointed in her direction. It had been impossible to see Holly's reaction when Gareth had leaned in to kiss her but the moment seemed to be over quite quickly. Megan despised herself for following them down to Mumbles. What on earth was I hoping to gain? she thought.

They were now heading in her direction and it looked as though they had decided to have lunch in Verdi's. She motioned to her waitress for the bill for the two cappuccinos she had lingered over while observing them. She needed to make a hasty exit; it wouldn't do to be caught spying. She paid in cash and slipped out of the side entrance, wishing she hadn't come.

CHAPTER 21

They had only been out of the house for forty-five minutes but, typically, the delivery had arrived in their absence. Helen could see the grey plastic outer packaging of the medium-sized parcel sitting on Carol's front doorstep as they rounded the corner at the end of the crescent. She was pretty sure it could only have been there for five or ten minutes. Any longer and, knowing Carol's neighbourhood, it would more than likely have disappeared.

It had only been six days since they'd posted the letter to Liberty Sands but, despite Helen's attempts to explain that it was unlikely that she would get a response so quickly, for the past few mornings Carol had been watching for the postman and had rushed into the hallway waiting for something to drop on the doormat. Each day she became more despondent and Helen realised she needed to do something to take Carol's mind off the wait for a reply. She had intended to start decorating Carol's bedroom when the weather got warmer so, without her knowledge, she had ordered some readymade curtains and a matching set of bedding online.

'What's that?' Carol asked, as the two women walked up the short path to the front door.

'It's a present from me to you.'

'What for? It's not my birthday.'

'I don't need a reason to buy you a gift,' Helen said, lifting the bulky square package. 'Come on, let's take it straight upstairs.'

Nobody had bought Carol a present of any description for years. She and Helen hadn't exchanged gifts at Christmas because she was out of the habit of celebrating Christmas and her birthday on Boxing Day. Helen had managed to persuade her to have a pre-lit tree on the table in the lounge and Carol grudgingly admitted she quite liked it, particularly when they were watching television in the evenings with the lights dimmed. Sometimes she had ignored the programmes on TV and sat staring at the white fairy lights, twinkling endlessly like stars in the night sky.

'Right,' Helen said, cutting open the plastic with the nail scissors she had grabbed from the bathroom on the way past, 'let's see if they're as good in real life as they looked on the Internet.' She shook out one of the duck-egg blue and ivory striped curtains and laid it on Carol's bed. 'What do you think? I think they look really fresh.'

She watched Carol look from the faded orange, water-stained rags, that framed the draughty old window, to the opulent fabric lying across her bed. A tear rolled from the corner of her eye as she stroked the fabric. 'They're beautiful,' she said. 'They remind me of summer.'

Helen was relieved. It was always difficult to gauge how Carol would react to something new because she was so resistant to change. 'They're lined as well,' she said, folding the fabric back to reveal a cream lining, 'so it should help to keep the draught from the windows out. I'll take the old curtains down and you have a look at the bedding set. I got you flannel. I thought it would feel softer against your skin.' She reached up to unhook the tatty old curtains. She could hear the rustle of cellophane and then silence. She unhooked the final curtain hook and let the dusty fabric fall to the floor. 'I'd have washed these ones but I don't think they would have survived a wash cycle in the machine,' she said, turning back to Carol. The older woman was sitting on the bed, tears streaming down her cheeks. 'What's the matter? Don't you like the new sheets?'

'Why are you doing this? I haven't got any money, you know,' Carol said. 'You're not going to be left a fortune in my will.'

'I don't want any money,' Helen said, crossing to the bed and kneeling down in front of Carol, taking hold of her hands and looking into the troubled grey eyes. 'I think life has been pretty rotten to you. You deserve to have someone show you kindness.'

'You're wrong, Helen. You don't know anything about me. I had my chance to be happy with Will and I repaid him by turning into a drunk. He should never have married me; he deserved so much better.' Tears ran freely down her cheeks and dropped on to the soft flannel sheets.

Helen was aching to put her arms around Carol. 'Will married you because he loved you. He must have seen in you what I see: a vulnerable frightened woman. He thought his love was enough to make you well, but you needed professional help. From what you told me the other day, I think you were suffering from post-natal depression after you had the baby. I'm just horrified that a health professional at the time didn't recognise it and try to get you help.'

'I didn't tell anyone how I was feeling. I was frightened they would take Holly away too and leave me with nothing again. It was selfish. I should have let them take her. I was an unfit mother.'

'Who did they take away from you Carol? Did you and Will have a baby before Holly?'

There it was. The question she had been longing to ask since she had arrived on Carol's doorstep.

'There was a baby, a girl,' Carol said, her brow knitted as though she was trying to remember. 'It was before I knew Will.'

'So, you had a boyfriend before you met Will, and he got you pregnant,' Helen gently coaxed.

'No. Will was my first boyfriend. I didn't talk to boys at school. I was too afraid in case he found out.'

'In case who found out, Carol?'

'My uncle. He said boys only wanted one thing from girls like me.'

Helen's palms were becoming clammy.

'They weren't supposed to find out. I was sent away to Aunty Ethel's when I started to get fat. They told my school I'd had a mental breakdown because of studying too hard for exams.'

'But you told me you'd never been back to Blackpool after your last holiday with your dad.'

Carol looked panicky. 'Did I? I must have forgotten.'

More likely so traumatised that she blanked it out, Helen thought. She knew she was on dangerous ground but she'd come too far to go back now. She had to know.

'So, if you didn't have a boyfriend, who was your baby's father?'

'Mummy told me I mustn't ever tell anyone. She said God would strike me dead if I kept telling such wicked lies. No one knew apart from her, not even Will, but she refused to believe that her brother would do such a thing.'

Helen shuddered. Not only had Carol's uncle George sexually abused his niece, he had got her pregnant and then tried to cover it up. But worse was the fact that Carol's mother had refused to see what was going on under her nose. How did she think her child had got pregnant? Immaculate conception? Helen had to breathe deeply to control her anger. When she had come looking for answers she had no idea of the desperately sad story she was going to uncover.

'How old were you when you had the baby?'

'I was thirteen. I had to go back to school after the Easter holidays and pretend nothing had happened. I was so scared one of the other girls would see the red marks on my stomach when we got changed for PE that I used to wear a vest. They teased me mercilessly. I used to get so hot that my face would be bright red all the time.'

Helen could barely ask the next question. 'So, what happened to your baby? Did your mum pretend it was hers?'

'No. Mummy didn't even want to see it. Aunty Ethel knew a childless couple who were too old to adopt. After she helped me give birth she cut the cord and handed my baby over to them. I wasn't even allowed to hold her; Aunty Ethel said it would be better that way. I cried for days. I was in so much pain because of the milk in my breasts. It wasn't Aunty Ethel's fault, she thought she was helping me, but I was ranting and raving at her so much that she called Uncle George to take me home. He was a very bad man. He said if I didn't calm down he would get the baby back and strangle it.'

Helen couldn't hold back any longer. She threw her arms around Carol and started hugging her. 'It's okay, it's all going to be okay.'

'What are you doing?' Carol shrieked, pushing Helen away from her so forcefully that she fell to the floor. 'Don't touch me. I don't like being touched. If you touch me again, I'll report you to social services. Get out of my room!' she screamed, *'Get out! GET OUT!'*

CHAPTER 22

'And wrapping in five, four, three, two, one,' the director's voice said in Holly's ear as Simon thanked her and threw to a commercial break.

'Two minutes, studio,' the floor manager said, ushering Holly off the sofa to replace her with the resident agony aunt, Lydia Lomax. 'Richard wants to see you upstairs,' he said, as Holly started to head for the dressing room.

'Now?' she asked.

'No, next Tuesday,' he snapped, shaking his head in disbelief. 'Yes, now,' he added, before muttering, 'bloody amateurs.'

Surely this isn't normal, Holly thought, as she made her way to the gallery. Why would Richard want to see me during the live broadcast? She wondered if she had been slightly less on it that morning, which would hardly have been surprising. Her mind was in turmoil after the attempted kiss from Gareth. She had no idea that he was still so in love with her. He had hidden it very well at Christmas when they had all stayed at Robert's but maybe that was because he knew that she was trying to make a go of things with Philippe. Although she hadn't told him the reason for her last-minute trip to Wales, it didn't take a rocket scientist to work out that all was not good between them.

The drive back from Wales had taken much longer than it should have because of an accident on the M4, so she had been late getting to Reading. She needed to unpack all her and Rosie's dirty clothes into the washing machine otherwise she wouldn't have the chance before the flight to Mexico on Saturday. She had also tried to ring Philippe, a phone call she had been dreading, but there was no reply, leaving her feeling agitated that she hadn't been able to sort out the situation before inevitably running into Maddie the next day. Then Rosie had filled her nappy, directly after having it changed, which had further delayed their departure for Woldingham, meaning that they had hit rush-hour traffic on the M25 and not arrived at Robert's until after 7 p.m. By the time she had fed and bathed Rosie and put her to bed it was nine o'clock before she and Robert sat down to dinner. Indigestion had kept her awake half the night, or was it indecision? She had no idea how she was going to handle future visits to Wales, if indeed there would be any, unless Harry was with her, and she still hadn't got hold of Philippe.

Yes, it's not really surprising if my performance on *On The Sofa* this morning wasn't quite up to scratch, she thought. Perhaps I'm going to get fired. Maybe that was how it happened in the world of television. No room for second chances. She tapped timidly at the door and pushed it open. Holly was still in awe of the people who worked on the technical side of producing *On The Sofa*. Not only did they have all the guests in the studio to deal with, they also had pre-recorded features to run into the show and live satellite broadcasts. Timings were crucial so, as they were in the middle of a count, Holly stayed quiet until she was spoken to.

Richard spun on his swivel chair to face her. 'How do you feel that went this morning?' he asked.

'Um, okay?' Holly replied.

'No, Holly, it wasn't okay.'

Holly could feel the colour rising in her cheeks. This was it. She was going to be fired from *On The Sofa* after just three appearances.

'It was bloody good. In fact, it was so bloody good that we don't want to drop the slot next week. Is there any possibility that you could fly back from your Mexico trip on Thursday so that you don't miss the show?'

Relief flooded through Holly. 'Well, um, I could try and change my flights I guess.'

'That's the correct answer. We'll pay any additional costs, of course. Do they fly you business class? If not, you'd better upgrade, we don't want you looking like a bag of shit on the sofa. There's only so much we can do with lights and make-up. Let Maddie know if you have any problem with it. By the way, don't go without seeing her, apparently you've got masses of fan mail. See you next week,' Richard said, turning back to the bank of monitors in front of him.

Holly slipped out of the gallery, closing the heavy door behind her and leant back against the corridor wall, her eyes closed. She had a thumping headache. Do I really need all this stress? she asked herself.

'Oh there you are. Is everything all right? It feels like you've been avoiding me this morning,' Maddie said.

Holly noted the accusation in her tone as she jolted upright. 'Oh, um, hi. Yes, everything's fine, I've just got a dreadful headache.'

'Follow me. There's a medicine cabinet in the make-up room. Let's get you some paracetamol. What did Richard want? Not a problem is there?'

'Not with the job – quite the opposite, in fact. Richard wants me to change my flight back from Mexico so that I won't miss next week's show. I don't think there'll be an issue. There are loads of flights to and from Mexico but I'm worried about taking Rosie on such a long flight if I'm only going to be there for three or four days. It doesn't seem fair to her.'

'Do you have to take her? Couldn't her dad look after her?'

'Actually, I'm not sure where he is,' Holly said, searching Maddie's face for any sign of guilt. 'I haven't been in touch with him since he got back from Dublin last week.'

'Dublin? Well, there's a coincidence, I was there last Thursday for my sister's wedding. Well, I say Dublin, we were out in the sticks somewhere. It took two hours to get there from the airport. That's why I missed my flight on the way back, the morning traffic was worse than London. I wish I'd known he was going to be there, maybe we could have met up for a drink or something.'

There was no hint of guile and no pretence that she wouldn't have tried to meet up with Philippe. Maddie was either a very practised liar or she genuinely hadn't known that he had been visiting Dublin at the same time as her.

'Have you got any pictures of the wedding?'

'Hundreds, but I'm not showing them to anybody. You

should have seen the bridesmaid dresses we had to wear. I always knew Ruby had no fashion sense but I hadn't realised quite how bad they were going to be.'

Holly was suspicious. Maddie was not the type to get embarrassed by a tasteless dress. It was more like her to hook her phone up to a TV monitor and give everyone a good laugh.

'Oh, come on, where's your sense of fun? I bet you looked amazing in it. You could make a bin liner look like haute couture,' Holly said, as they entered the make-up room.

'If you're hoping to persuade her to show you photos of the wedding you can forget it. We've been trying all week and she's not having any of it,' Tamsin said. 'I'm starting to doubt that her sister got married after all. Maybe Maddie just had a hot date and the family wedding was an excuse so that Richard would give her the time off.'

Holly was watching Maddie carefully. She didn't bat an eyelid. She really was a cool customer. After reaching into the medicine cabinet for the paracetamol and filling a glass with water from the tap, she handed them to Holly.

'Okay,' she said, 'you win. But if any of these images mysteriously find their way on to social media I will not be responsible for my actions.'

Holly's throat was so tight she could barely swallow the pills. If Maddie really had been at her sister's wedding on the Thursday night, miles from anywhere, she couldn't have been having passionate sex with Philippe.

Tamsin screeched. 'Oh my God! Who has lime green puffball dresses for their bridesmaids?'

'My sister, unfortunately,' said Maddie. 'As you can see there were eight of us. We looked like a pod of underripe peas with arms and legs and heads. This is sooo embarrassing.'

Holly was peering over Maddie's shoulder as she scrolled through shot after shot of the bridesmaids in their hideous outfits getting increasingly drunk at the reception. It would seem that Holly had jumped to the wrong conclusion about Maddie and Philippe after all. Thank goodness I didn't confront him with my suspicions, she thought. He must have been wondering why I wasn't answering his calls and messages.

'Shit! The ring,' she said, out loud, before she could stop herself.

'You've got good eyesight to notice the ring,' Tamsin said.

'Actually, I thought the ring was the best thing about her whole wedding outfit, and I'm guessing that's because Kealan chose it,' Maddie said.

'Th-that's what I meant,' Holly lied, colouring up furiously, 'I'm surprised at how lovely it is.'

'Right, so if you two have sufficiently embarrassed me, I'll just fetch Holly's fan mail. I think Annabel's nose is a bit out of joint. You had twice the amount she did this week, Holly.'

Holly wasn't listening. She had sent Philippe his ring back in a fit of pique and now he wasn't answering her calls. She had really blown it this time.

CHAPTER 23

Philippe rolled over in the crisp white hotel sheets and pulled one of the spare pillows over his face. It did nothing to deaden the noise of the incessant car horns, which were ear-splittingly loud, even with the double-glazed balcony doors closed, and he could almost taste the petrol fumes that permeated the air. Coming here, amid all the hustle and bustle, may not have been the wisest decision after all, he thought.

When he had stormed out of Jo's office four days earlier, he had only one thing on his mind. He had to confront Holly and find out what the hell was going on. She had clearly been avoiding his calls and had returned the engagement ring with no message in the package. Had she had met someone else? Perhaps the producer of *On The Sofa* had shown some interest in her and she had fallen for his charm. Maybe getting her the job in television wasn't such a smart move; everyone knew what these 'telly types' were like. Holly was so inexperienced in relationships she may have succumbed to a bit of attention and some sweet-talking. It would be almost a carbon copy of what had happened between them in

Mauritius, except that he really did love Holly and he had thought that she felt the same way.

He didn't want to embarrass himself or Holly by turning up on her doorstep in Reading if she had someone else there, so he had decided to book a flight to Mexico. He knew which resort and hotel she was going to be reviewing for her latest Liberty Sands piece so he planned to arrive a couple of days before her and that way her cover story would remain intact. No one would be aware that they already knew each other and she wouldn't be able to run away because she was working. He had given her the time and space she had asked for, the very least he expected in return was a few words of explanation, not just a returned ring in a padded envelope.

He had to talk things through with Holly. The situation between them was unresolved, and was starting to affect all areas of his life, especially his work. Jo wasn't the most sympathetic editor in the world and, despite his success, she could get difficult if he didn't start meeting at least some of his deadlines. Devastating though it would be if Holly was interested in someone else, he needed to know why she had abruptly stopped answering his calls and why she had sent the ring back. Surely that wasn't unreasonable he had persuaded himself as he picked up the phone to talk to a travel company that specialised in last-minute bookings.

In the back of a London black cab on his way to Heathrow Airport, Philippe started to have doubts. Maybe it was a test? Perhaps Holly had returned the ring to see how he would react and he had no idea what she expected his reaction to be. Why did women have to be so complicated? Philippe had never chased a woman before in his life. He hadn't needed to but, more importantly, he hadn't wanted to. Although some things are worth fighting for, there must come a time when you just have to accept defeat. Maybe Holly didn't love him as much as he loved her and had only given him a second chance because of Rosie, but had now realised that wasn't enough to sustain a relationship, a marriage even.

Philippe reached a decision as the cab pulled up outside the terminal building. His bag was packed and maybe a break would bring him the inspiration he so desperately needed for his new book. He checked the departures board and then rang the travel company.

'Hi, I'm sorry to bother you again but I've changed my mind about Mexico. Can you get me on a flight to Cuba today? I'm at Heathrow now so I'll wait here for you to confirm.'

The travel company had been very efficient in booking his new destination and, despite them being unable to offer any kind of refund because of the late cancellation, he had no complaints. Five hours later he was on a flight to Cuba with a hotel booked in central Havana. They had tried to persuade him to stay in Varadero, the tourist area, but the last thing Philippe wanted was to be surrounded by couples and families with young children. That would just be rubbing salt into an open wound.

He emerged from under the soft, marshmallow-like pillow and crossed to the windows. The cacophony doubled in volume as he slid the doors open and stepped out on to the balcony, breathing in the warm air polluted with petrol fumes. He had always wanted to visit Cuba, famed for the old American cars that had long since disappeared from the streets of New York and the highways of Florida, and, of course, cigars. Philippe wouldn't class himself as a smoker but he could picture himself now inhaling the tobacco smell while rolling a fat cigar between his fingers and sipping on the brandy in his other hand. I could murder a drink, he thought, looking longingly at the minibar in his room.

CHAPTER 24

Holly slid on to the back seat of the waiting car, dropping the heavy plastic bag containing her fan mail into the foot well of the seat next to her. Fan mail for little old me, she thought, that is just weird. What a shame there won't be any time to have a look at that before I head off to Mexico tomorrow, but I will read and reply to every person who's taken the trouble to write to me. Well, maybe not every person.

Maddie had warned her that there would probably be some hate mail in with the adoring letters and, inevitably, some from nutters.

'We used to have staff to vet all the fan mail,' she explained, 'but since budgets have been cut, it's a case of the on-air talent taking them home or they go in the shredder.'

Holly fervently hoped there wouldn't be too many nasty letters but she couldn't bear the thought of all the nice letters going unread.

'I'll be fine, Maddie,' she said. 'I promise I won't take any of them too seriously.'

Maddie raised her eyebrows. 'You'd do well to

remember that promise because the funny thing is, you always remember the nasty ones, even when the ratio is one bad letter to a hundred good.'

As the car slid out into the London traffic, Holly eyed the bag, wondering whether to read a few on her way back to Woldingham. She decided against it and instead picked up her mobile phone.

'Hi Harry, it's Mum.'

'I know, Mum, your number came up. I probably wouldn't have answered if it hadn't been you. We were just watching you on the telly again instead of revising. It'll be your fault if we flunk our exams.'

'We?' Holly said. 'Don't tell me you made poor old Hugo and Jack watch too?'

'No, I'm at Amy's. She invited me round so that we could watch it together. I haven't actually told anyone else that you're doing it. You're not cross, are you?'

'Of course not. Let's face it, it might be very short-lived and then it would be embarrassing for you to explain. Television is so fickle. One minute you're flavour of the month and the next minute no one wants to know you. In fact, I thought I was going to be fired this morning.'

'Why? What happened? Is everything okay?'

'Yes, it's fine. I just wanted your opinion about something but it doesn't matter if you're busy.'

'Never too busy for you, Mum, fire away.'

'Well, you know I'm off to Mexico tomorrow. It was meant to be for a week but *On The Sofa* have asked me to come back early so that I don't miss next week's show.'

'Blimey, that's brilliant! You're already indispensable.'

'I wouldn't say that exactly but it is a nice compliment. The trouble is, I don't really want to take Rosie all that way for five days. Seven is bad enough, what with jet lag, change of climate and the flight itself, of course, but five would really unsettle her.'

'Do you want me to come home for a few days?'

'Well, that's one option but I don't want to interfere with your revision. What do you think about me asking Robert to have her?'

'Um, I'm not sure about that, Mum. I know he loves her to bits but he's never been around young babies full-time. He's fine when you're there to hand her back to, but what if she wasn't well? I think it's a big ask.'

'That's what I thought, although he has got Nick virtually living at the house now and he's had plenty of experience with babies.'

'Not with Rosie, though, and it is a bit of an imposition. You barely know him.'

'You're right. I guess I'll have to take her with me as I'd originally planned.'

'Hang on a minute.'

Holly was aware of slightly muffled voices, as though Harry had put his hand over the phone.

'Right, so Amy says she'll come back to Reading with me. If we're both there we can take it in turns to revise and babysit Rosie.'

'Are you sure? Isn't that almost as bad as expecting Nick to muck in and help?'

'Hardly, Mum. I've known Amy for nearly three years and she knows you and she's babysat Rosie with me before. We'll be fine. I think you're right that the trip would be too much for Rosie and I'm presuming you don't want to hand her over to her father?'

It might help if I knew where he was, Holly thought.

'No. He's had even less experience with small babies than Robert.' Holly felt a prick of conscience: one reason Philippe was so inexperienced with small babies was because she had barely allowed him to see his daughter. I really have to sort things out with him, she thought, before I lose him once and for all.

'Amy and me it is then. What time is your flight tomorrow?'

'Not until the evening, thank goodness.'

'We'll come up around midday.'

'Thanks, Harry. Amy really is so kind. See you both tomorrow.'

Holly disconnected the call, wondering for the umpteenth time what was stopping her son and Amy from going out with each other when they were clearly such a good match. Amy had been split up from Jack for nine months now and, according to Harry, had not been seeing anyone else so what was holding them back? Although she had told Robert not to meddle she was sorely tempted to do so herself. Who knows, she thought, maybe the two of them playing happy families with Rosie might be the catalyst for them to at least start dating.

Holly was pleased with the decision that Harry had helped her reach regarding Rosie, and again marvelled at his maturity. Maybe I should ask his advice about Philippe? she mused, he certainly seems able to see both sides of a situation better than I do. Perhaps being the child of a single parent has its advantages after all.

She was just about to slip her phone back into her bag when it started ringing. Assuming it must be Harry calling to check some detail with her she answered it. 'I hope you haven't changed your mind?'

'About what?'

Holly caught her breath. It was Jo. She hadn't spoken to her at all since the night in October when Rosie was born prematurely.

'Hello, Jo,' Holly said, recovering her composure. 'Long time no speak.'

Jo ignored the dig. 'Who did you think was calling? Philippe? Is he being indecisive again?'

'No, I had been talking to my son, so I assumed he'd forgotten to ask me something.'

'Oh yes, your secret son, Harry. I can't believe you didn't tell me about him. I thought we were supposed to be friends.'

'We were supposed to be friends, Jo, but the situation has changed since your behaviour at Mosiman's. I could have lost Rosie that night. I was only thirty-two weeks pregnant, she might not have survived, and for what? So that you could have your moment of vindictive pleasure?'

There was a pause.

'Actually, Holly, that's why I'm ringing. I wanted to apologise for my actions that night. You must have had your reasons for keeping secrets from me and I should have respected that.'

Am I hearing things? she thought. Jo has rung to apologise to me? Jo never apologises to anyone.

'Are you busy on Monday?' Jo continued. 'I'd like to take you to lunch.'

What is she up to? Holly wondered. This is completely out of character.

'Actually, I have one of my Liberty Sands trips to go on tomorrow and I won't be back until next Thursday.'

'Oh yes, another little secret you were keeping from

me. But surely you've blown that now that you're on television? Everyone will recognise you so you won't be able to travel incognito any more. Where are you off to this time?' she added, casually.

'The Mayan Riviera in Mexico. I'm pretty sure most of the local staff there won't watch *On The Sofa*. But you're right, some of the holidaymakers might. It's a "suck it and see" situation. If I keep being recognised when I'm supposed to be undercover, Soleil will probably pull the plug. Knowing my luck, that will be at the same time as *On The Sofa* decide I'm not for them and I will be back to square one, but without the copy-editing work you used to send me.'

'I didn't think you'd have the time for any copy-editing work with the new baby. It's something we can discuss at lunch if you're still interested in it. How about a week on Monday instead? I'll even let you choose the restaurant.'

Holly didn't really want to go for lunch with Jo. She had seen a side to her at Mosiman's that she didn't like, but she couldn't afford to be too choosy about who she accepted work from. Jo knew a lot of people in the publishing industry, and a few words like 'unreliable' or 'difficult' bandied around, however unjustly, could stop her getting work elsewhere.

'Okay, but you choose the restaurant, I don't know many posh places in London,' she said, deliberately emphasising the word posh. If I'm going to have lunch with Jo at least I'll have the satisfaction of knowing that it's cost a small fortune, she thought.

'What about Langan's? It's one of Philippe's favourites.'

'Oh, I didn't realise the invitation was for both of us,' Holly faltered. 'You'll have to invite him yourself, I'm afraid. He's not answering my calls at the moment.' As soon the words were out of her mouth she regretted them. She could imagine the smug expression on Jo's face.

'No, no. The invitation is just for you, I was merely commenting that it's one of Philippe's favourite haunts and we all know what impeccable taste he has.' Was Holly imagining it, or had a note of sarcasm dripped into Jo's voice? 'Shall we say one o'clock? I look forward to a proper catch up and I might have an interesting proposition for you,' she added, before saying her goodbyes.

Holly felt like she had just done two rounds with Mike Tyson. Jo really was a slippery customer and what the hell did that last comment mean? She had no time to give it any further thought as the car was already pulling into Robert's driveway and she couldn't wait to get her hands on Rosie for a cuddle, particularly as they were going to be spending the next five days apart for the first time.

CHAPTER 25

Once again, Carol had been transfixed as she watched Liberty Sands on television that morning. Helen's eyes were drawn from one woman to the other. What a tragedy that a sequence of events in her early life had prevented Carol from forming a proper bond with the woman who was lighting up the TV screen. She was a real beauty, Helen thought, bearing no resemblance to her mother, but was the image of her dead father. They had gone through most of the photographs from the loft and each time there was one of Holly and Will together, Helen became more certain that Holly was Liberty. She wondered if Carol's letter had been opened yet and, if so, what Holly's reaction had been. She hoped that Holly would be able to forgive her mum for the terrible things she had done, before it was too late.

Directly after the Liberty Sands slot, Carol had excused herself, saying she was tired and was going for a lie down. She seemed to be fading before Helen's eyes. She was picking at her food again and seemed to have lost the desire to do anything, spending more and more time in her room alone. There was definitely a smell of alcohol on her breath each time she emerged, which scared Helen. The cirrhosis was quite advanced and the doctors had been very specific that her liver would be unable to cope with much more abuse.

Helen couldn't understand where Carol was getting the alcohol from. She didn't go anywhere on her own so she couldn't be buying whisky and bringing it into the house, and the only time she was left alone was if Helen nipped out to the local shops without her. Someone must be supplying her with it, but who? And where was she hiding it? It must be somewhere in her room, Helen thought, but she hadn't come across it the previous day when she was hanging the new curtains and putting the new linen on the bed.

Carol had emerged from her room about an hour after her outburst, completely calm and seemingly with no recollection of the incident. She merely wanted to know what her curtains were doing in a heap on the floor. Helen had been preparing a salad for their lunch but went back upstairs to finish off the job she had started an hour before, leaving Carol in the kitchen to butter some bread. She checked the wardrobe and chest of drawers for bottles of whisky but drew a blank. She even checked inside Carol's boots, pushed under her old wooden dressing table in the corner of the room, but to no avail.

So, Helen had come up with a plan. After lunch, she was going to pretend to leave the house to go to the shops, but instead was going to hide in her room and try to catch the culprit. Surely whoever is doing it must realise that they are killing her, she thought, even if it is out of misplaced kindness.

The leeks, garlic and potatoes had been bubbling away

in vegetable stock for twenty minutes. Helen plugged in the handheld blender in readiness for liquidising the soup and went to the foot of the stairs.

'Carol, lunch is almost ready,' she called, before going back into the kitchen and submerging the blender into the boiling liquid. She moved it slowly around the pan, watching the vortex created as the chunky vegetables were drawn on to the blades. Within two minutes the soup was smooth and creamy, and light green in colour. She popped the lid back on the saucepan and rinsed the blender under the hot tap. The bowls were sitting on the work surface waiting to be filled, along with a plate of torn bits of unbuttered French bread.

'Carol,' she called again. 'Come on or it will get cold. It's leek and potato soup. Your favourite.'

There was no response.

Helen flicked the gas off under the saucepan before climbing the stairs to find out what was keeping Carol. She knocked lightly on her bedroom door and then turned the knob and pushed the door open. An involuntary scream emitted from her. Carol was lying facedown, sprawled across the bed, with a bottle of pills in her hand and an almost empty bottle of whisky balancing precariously on the edge of the bed, the remainder of its pungent contents dripping rhythmically on to the threadbare carpet.

Resisting the urge to touch anything, Helen ran down the stairs and dialled 999.

'Ambulance, and please hurry. I think my mother's dying.'

CHAPTER 26

'She's going to be fine. Stop fussing.'

'I'm sorry,' Holly said, 'it's just that I've never left her for more than a few hours before.'

'To be brutally honest, Mum, you are going to miss Rosie way more than she is going to miss you. So long as she has food, and cuddles from people she knows, she won't even realise you're not here. Hand her over and go and put that poor cab driver out of his misery, he's been waiting twenty minutes already.'

Holly brushed a tear away from the corner of her eye and planted a kiss on Rosie's forehead before she reluctantly handed her over to Harry.

'Be a good girl for your big brother,' she said, as she closed the front door behind her without a backward glance.

'Phew, your poor mum. That must have been so difficult for her. I hope you were just being cruel to be kind when you said Rosie wouldn't miss her mum because she will, you know.'

'Of course she will but it wouldn't have benefited anybody for Mum to get too emotional.'

'Do you think she'll be all right?' Amy asked, as she closed the curtains after the Toyota Prius had pulled away from the kerb.

'Well, she'll be shedding a few tears in the back of the taxi right now but she'll cope, she always does. I think she's going to have to reconsider the Soleil job though. It was perfect when it was just her, but I really can't see how it's going to work now this little madam has joined us,' Harry said, affectionately rubbing his nose against Rosie's. 'Let's hope the producers at *On The Sofa* will give her a longer contract soon and then she'll be able to relax a bit and maybe someone else can become Liberty Sands. Right, princess, let's get your bottle and take you up to bed and then Aunty Amy and I can have some dinner.'

'Do you need a hand?'

'I've had plenty of practice in that department, thanks,' Harry said, wrinkling his nose. 'Why don't you put the pizza in the oven in about ten minutes and then we can settle down to some Saturday night television? If you want garlic bread there's some in the freezer,' Harry added, heading up the stairs with his sister reaching impatiently for the bottle of warm milk in his hand.

Half an hour later, Harry leaned back on the sofa patting his stomach, a satisfied expression on his face. 'That hit the spot nicely,' he said. 'I didn't realise you could cook, Amy.'

'That's because you always insist on doing it cos you're so damn good at it. Anyway, heating up a pizza can hardly be classed as cordon bleu. I might go crazy and make you one of my famous quiches while we're here, or a risotto.

Which would you prefer?'

'Either. I like most food really, apart from kebabs. I'm always worried about how long the meat has been there and how many times it's been reheated. Risotto sounds good.'

'Okay, we can have that on Monday. I thought maybe we could have a traditional roast dinner tomorrow if you fancy. It's one of my favourites, but there's been precious little opportunity while I've been at uni cos I've always been helping Geoff in the bookshop on Sundays.'

'How is Geoff? Is he over his fling with Jo? I can't understand what on earth he saw in the woman if I'm honest.'

'Love's a funny thing. Sometimes we let our hearts rule our heads and we choose people that we're not really suited to.'

Harry seized the opportunity. 'Is that what happened with you and Jack? I must admit I was surprised you two broke things off so suddenly. I know you didn't always agree on stuff but you both seemed pretty happy. He hasn't been much fun to be around since you moved out.'

'It wasn't solely my decision, Harry. We both agreed that we needed time apart. It's just turned out that I wasn't the right person for Jack after all and maybe he wasn't the right man for me either. I've told you before, it's off limits. I don't want to talk about it.'

Harry looked across at Amy snuggled into the corner of his sofa. Whenever he had tried to broach the subject of her and Jack she clammed up. Jack was the same. He had point-blank refused to talk about it to Hugo and Harry, although he had volunteered to pay Amy's share of the rent. Hugo had immediately told him not to be such an arse, offering to pay the extra because he could afford it better, but in the end they had agreed to split things three ways, which seemed the fairest option. It was weird to think that pretty soon they would be giving up the flat and heading off in different directions.

'If you change your mind, I'm here, and I'm a very good listener.'

'I know. You've always been there for me.' Just not in the way I wanted, she added silently. 'So, what shall we watch? There must be some kind of talent show on?'

'Of course. Typical Saturday night banality. I don't mind the acts so much, it's the judges trying to compete for airtime that drives me mad. We could watch a film if you prefer? Mum's got a few decent DVDs.'

'I'm easy. You choose, I'll probably fall asleep anyway. Apologies in advance if I do but it's been a busy week. To be honest, I was really glad of the chance to get away from Bath for a few days. Everyone is so stressed out with exams looming.'

'I hope you're still saying that at six in the morning when Rosie wakes up for her morning feed,' Harry said, slipping the shiny round disc of Zoolander into the DVD player. 'Have you seen this before? I love Ben Stiller and his "blue steel" look.' He contorted his features into a pretty passable impression.

Amy laughed. 'It's one of my favourites too although, I must confess, I prefer Owen Wilson. I always have had a preference for blonds,' she said, colouring slightly, as she thought of Jack's raven dark hair.

CHAPTER 27

The relatives' room was warm and stuffy. Helen sat on the uncomfortable olive green leatherette chair, her elbows resting on her knees and her face in her hands, sobbing quietly. When Carol had been admitted to hospital two hours previously, Helen had been asked what her relationship with the patient was. For the first time in her life she had uttered the words, 'She's my mother.'

'Do you know if she has taken any medication?' was the next question.

Helen handed over the empty pill bottle. The receptionist raised her eyebrows.

'Do you know how many of these she has taken?'

Helen shook her head, 'No, but they were washed down with whisky.'

'She's in a bad way, but hopefully we got to her in time. If you take a seat in the relatives' room, I'll update you as soon as I have any news.'

Helen had been waiting, all alone, ever since. All she could think was, 'Please don't let her die.' Her decision not to reveal her true identity to Carol when she had taken the role as her live-in carer was preying on her mind. Helen had only discovered she was adopted two years previously when a guilt ridden Aunty Ethel had a bout of conscience on her death bed. She had written to Helen at her parents' former address, giving the name of her real mother, and the letter had been forwarded on. Initially, Helen needed to be certain that Carol was her birth mother, but she also wanted to find out who her father was. She feared the truth may not be forthcoming once Carol knew that Helen was the illegitimate baby who had been taken away from her when she was only thirteen. Helen had been on the verge of telling Carol what their real relationship was on several occasions but it had proved more difficult to find the words than she had imagined. Then Liberty Sands, aka Holly, had appeared out of the blue on their television screen and had derailed her plans. Carol's obsession for getting in touch with Holly to apologise had taken precedence over everything else and Helen had decided it wouldn't have been good for her health to deliver another shock too soon. She was so frail and confused because of the dementia and, according to her doctor, living on borrowed time because of the massive damage she had caused to her liver through years of alcohol abuse, that Helen had decided her revelation would have to wait.

'Why didn't I just tell her?' she said to herself. 'This might never have happened if I'd told her straightaway who I am.'

The noise of a throat being cleared caused Helen to look up. A young nurse stood in the doorway. She could only have been around twenty years old and her face was pale and serious.

'Are you Mrs Richardson?' she asked, tentatively.

'Is she…?' Helen couldn't finish her sentence.

'We've managed to stabilise your mother for now, but she's in a bad way. If you have any other family members you'd like to visit her, you should call them to come as soon as possible.'

'What are you saying? Is she going to die?'

'I'm not qualified to say. I'm only passing on what the doctor has just told me. They had to pump your mother's stomach and for someone in such poor physical condition as your mother is it's a huge trauma. It might just be precautionary but, if there is anyone else, you should contact them.'

'Can I see her?'

'She's in recovery but I'll come and fetch you as soon as we move her on to a ward. Have you had a cup of tea?'

Helen shook her head, the thought of it making her feel physically sick. 'No, I don't want anything.'

'Well, if you change your mind, come to the nurses' station and we can organise it for you.'

'Thank you,' Helen muttered, her head dropping back into her hands. The one person she desperately needed to reach was Holly. Carol was unaware that Helen had slipped a message of her own into the envelope, along with the letter and photograph, before sealing it and sending it to the television studios. Surely if Holly had seen it she would have been in touch? Carol hadn't been the best mother in the world but she was still her mother, her own flesh and blood. Did I write enough to persuade her to at least contact us?

Dear Holly/Liberty

Please don't dismiss this letter without reading it. I work as your mother's carer and I know how dreadfully she treated you in childhood and after your father's death but there is a terrible reason behind all this that I have discovered. Your mother is now suffering from dementia and cirrhosis of the liver. She may not have much longer to live and I believe she wants to go to her grave knowing that she has at least had the chance to say she's sorry. Please contact her, she is desperate to see you. You should also know that she is immensely proud of you.

Kind Regards
Helen Richardson

Although Holly wouldn't appear on *On The Sofa* for another six days, Helen had to make contact with Holly before then. She would ring the production office at the television studios first thing on Monday morning, if Carol lasted that long, she thought, a shiver running through her body.

CHAPTER 28

Harry's hands were shaking as he reread the final line of the letter his grandmother had written to her estranged daughter. He felt guilty that he was seeing the words before his mother had chance to but, under the circumstances, he thought it was the right thing to do. The photo of his mum as a young teenager smiling up at her dad, whom she so closely resembled, lay on the coffee table next to a note from his grandmother's carer. On the floor there were two neat piles of opened and discarded letters.

He had been in the middle of giving Rosie her breakfast when the phone had rung at 8.15 that morning.

'Amy, are you okay to get that?' he called. 'It's probably Mum miscalculating the time difference between Mexico and the UK.'

'Got it,' Amy called back.

A few minutes later she walked into the kitchen looking pale and shocked.

'What's wrong?' Harry was immediately concerned. 'Is Mum all right?'

'It wasn't your mum, Harry, it was Maddie from the

television studios.'

Relief was replaced by anxiety. 'Why are they ringing here? They know she's away in Mexico until Thursday.'

'Maddie said that they had received a dozen or more phone calls, since six o' clock this morning, from a woman who claims that the lady in her care recognised Liberty Sands on the television and insists she is her long-lost daughter. Apparently crank calls aren't that unusual, but this woman's persistence and the fact that she knew your mum's real name is Holly Wilson made Maddie wonder if she was telling the truth. The carer said that Holly's mother is in hospital in a critical condition after some kind of drug overdose, which she claims was brought on because Holly hadn't replied to a letter sent in to the studios ten days ago.'

'A letter? Do you think it's in that bag of fan mail that Mum hasn't had time to look at yet?' Harry said, scraping the last of the baby porridge from the bowl and spooning it into Rosie's mouth.

'Maybe,' Amy replied. 'This woman must be very impatient. Ten days isn't exactly a long time to wait for a reply from someone off the television. I remember sending a Valentine card to one of the members of Blue when I was about seven. I think I got the compliment slip and a signed photo during the school summer holidays, by which time I'd gone off him and moved on to liking someone in Westlife. Do you think she really is Holly's mum?'

'If they'd said she was in hospital with an alcohol-related problem, I'd be inclined to believe it. Mum hasn't spoken to me much about her mother except to say she was an alcoholic who didn't want us in her life. I don't know, Amy. Maybe there is something in this. It hasn't been widely broadcast that Liberty Sands' real name is Holly Wilson. Perhaps we should look for the letter and see what it says. What do you think?' Harry asked, lifting his baby sister out of her high chair and cuddling her in the crook of his arm to feed her a bottle of warm formula.

'I think you'll make a perfect dad, one day,' Amy said, unable to stop herself saying exactly what she had been thinking.

'About looking for the letter?' Harry said, without raising his gaze from Rosie. 'If it genuinely is Mum's mother trying to make contact she may well have written something awful. She was pretty vile to my mum when she found out she was pregnant with me.'

'Well, I'm happy to help you search through the letters if you think your mum won't mind,' Amy said. 'She told me she was a bit concerned about getting hate mail so, in a way, we'd be doing her a favour by filtering any unpleasant stuff out. What will you do if we find this woman's letter though?'

'Good question. There's not much point in worrying Mum with it while she's so far away but, on the other hand, I'd feel pretty crappy if my grandmother was trying to build bridges and something happened to her before Mum got back. I think we need to read what she has written before deciding whether to tell Mum or not.'

'I agree. I'll make us some toast and then we can make a start. Rosie's such a little sweetheart she'll keep herself amused with her activity mat now that she's had something to eat.'

Neither Harry nor Amy had come across any nasty letters for Holly. Harry was glowing with pride as he read the endless compliments that unknown fans were showering on her. Occasionally, he would mutter, 'Gross, that's my mum you're fantasising about.'

Amy had sorted the letters into two piles so they could make quicker progress. As she opened one envelope, a photograph fell to the floor. They both looked down at the picture and knew that they'd found the letter. Harry picked the photograph up and gazed at it for a few moments before laying it down on the coffee table and taking the letter from Amy's extended hand. The writing was a barely legible scrawl, as though the writer's shaking hands had made controlling a pen difficult.

Dear Liberty

I'm glad you changed your name. I never did like the name Holly, that was your father's choice. I was surprised to see you on the television but I knew straight away that it was you, even with your new name. You haven't really changed much after all this time but it was when I heard your voice that I knew for sure that it was you. You look happy and believe it or not that makes me happy. I know I have not been a good mother to you and for that I am truly sorry. I wanted to love you, really I did, but something deep inside kept stopping me. I used to cry myself to sleep at night because you never hugged me the same way that you hugged your dad. Even as a baby I think you were a little scared of me, and you were right to be. I'm not going to make excuses about the way I've treated you.

I have needlessly punished myself by cutting you out of my life and never wanting to see my grandson. Does he look like you and your dad? I blamed you for taking away the tiny bit of happiness I had in my life when your father was killed in the crash. I've had time, so much time, to reflect and it's now clear to me that he wouldn't have died that night if I hadn't forced him into seeing you and your baby secretly. Regret doesn't come close to explaining how I feel about all the years I've wasted not having you in my life. I'm paying for all the mistakes I've made. I'm a sad lonely old woman with only a carer for company. I crave the drink that has destroyed me even as I sit writing this to you. It numbs the pain of reality. Sometimes I can't remember things, people's names or faces, but you and your dad are always clear to me. So many times I have gone to bed at night praying that I won't wake up for another day of torment but now I'm frightened that I might die before I can tell you how very very sorry I am. I wish our lives together could have been different but I can't change the past and the terrible things I've said to you. My wish is to see you before I die and to apologise to you face to face but I can't even promise that if I were to see you again I wouldn't be just as cruel and I do understand if you never want to lay eyes on me again. Why would you? Pray for me Holly, yes, I'm using your given name, because I think I will spend my eternity in Hell.

If you can find forgiveness in your heart you know where I am and if you come, please bring the boy.

Mum (Carol)

Harry was aware of Amy watching him, her face a mix of anxiety and concern. Slowly he handed the letter over to her.

'It wasn't what I was expecting,' he said, his voice thick with emotion. 'Actually, I don't know what I was expecting. I've spent my life alternating between hate and indifference towards a person who, by the sound of this letter, needed help desperately. She sounds so... so defeated, Amy. I hope Mum will be able to forgive her.'

A fat tear rolled down Amy's cheek.

'You need to read the note from her carer as well. It sounds as though there must have been a terrible catalyst early on in her life that destroyed her ability to love. I can't imagine what it must be like to not be able to love, even if the person doesn't love you in return.' Another tear rolled off the end of her nose and fell noiselessly on the carpet.

'You mean Jack? You're obviously still in love with him. You have to talk to someone about it.'

'I don't mean Jack,' Amy said, overcome by the emotion of the moment. 'It's you Harry. It's always been you.'

There was silence. Even Rosie stopped gurgling as though stunned by Amy's admission.

'I'm sorry; I shouldn't have said that. This isn't the right time. How selfish of me. You've just had your first ever contact with your grandmother and I'm burdening you with my problems,' she rambled.

'Stop talking, Amy,' Harry said, closing his eyes.

'I don't know why I said that. Please try and forget it. We're friends, right? I don't want anything I've just said to change that. I was trying to get to the end of uni without you ever knowing how I feel about you and then

149

I planned to go off travelling the world in the hope that I would find someone to stop me loving you.'

Harry was silent.

'Harry? Please say something. You're my best friend in the world. I couldn't bear it if this comes between us.'

Harry could feel the rhythmic thudding of his heart. He and Amy were as close as two people could be outside of a relationship. They were completely comfortable in each other's company. Apart from his mum, and now his baby sister, she was the person he cared most about in the world. He adored her. So what am I so afraid of? he thought. In the early days at Bath, why did I push her away and straight into Jack's arms? Jack had always said he couldn't believe his luck when Amy had agreed to start dating. 'I thought it was you she was soft on,' he had confessed, on more than one occasion. So was their whole relationship a lie? Harry thought, his eyes suddenly snapping open. Amy was staring at him.

'But you chose Jack.'

Amy inhaled deeply. 'You can only make a choice when there is more than one thing on offer. I was plump and ginger. No one ever paid me any attention, particularly not someone like you. You weren't interested in me and Jack was. I – I guess I was flattered by the attention and I really liked his sense of fun. I grew to love him but I always knew he wasn't the person I would spend the rest of my life with. Does that make me a bad person?'

'So you eventually found the courage to break things off with him?'

'No. Well, yes. Ultimately I did finish things between us. Something happened. I can't talk about it because I promised Jack I wouldn't and I owe him that much.'

'Did he cheat on you? I'll break his scrawny neck if he did.'

'No, not exactly. He – he had feelings for someone else. Please don't ask me any more questions about it. Jack will tell you himself when he's ready. It all came to a head at Hugo's house in Barbados and that's why I moved out of the flat at the start of term. Don't say anything to Jack, will you.'

'Is he gay?'

Amy's cheeks flushed.

'He is, isn't he. I did wonder when we first met but when he started dating you I just assumed I'd got it wrong. Why doesn't he just admit it? No one bats an eyelid these days.'

'I'm not saying you're right or wrong, Harry. Jack's sexuality is his business. I think he hasn't said anything because he wanted to protect me. Some of the girls can be really bitchy, particularly the ones who think our friendship stops you dating other girls. They'd love spreading the gossip I was so crap in bed that I'd turned my boyfriend gay – not that I'm saying he is.'

'I won't say anything to him, but I wish he could have trusted Hugo and me enough to confide in us. Is he seeing somebody?'

'I don't know. Don't look at me like that, Harry, I really don't know. We haven't spoken in ages. There was the guy that he fancied when he was still with me but I don't know if he has taken things any further. Can we stop talking about this now? I feel dreadful about telling you.'

'You didn't tell me, I guessed. Poor Amy, that's a hell of a secret to be carrying around.'

'Two secrets, Harry, and now they are both out in the

open. Shall I go and pack my things? You'll be able to manage Rosie on your own until your mum gets back I'm sure.'

'Do you want to leave?'

Amy shook her head.

'Then don't.' Harry moved from the armchair to sit next to Amy on the sofa. He put his arm around her shoulder and pulled her in towards his chest, resting his chin on the top of her head. 'I'd like you to stay.'

'Really? You're not just saying that because you feel sorry for me?'

Harry lifted her face so that he could look into her eyes that harboured a mix of love and hope. He gently kissed her. For the first time in his life he experienced the feeling of fireworks exploding in his chest. 'What do you think?' he asked. He leaned in to kiss her again, this time with more passion and urgency.

With immaculate timing, his iPad started ringing. He pulled away from Amy and picked it up.

'It's Mum. She wants to Facetime. What am I going to say?'

'You have to tell her about the letter, Harry. Your mum's a grown woman, she'll have to make her own decisions as to whether to come back early from Mexico or not.'

Harry nodded and pressed accept.

CHAPTER 29

Philippe raised his gaze from the computer screen, where words seemed to be swimming in front of his tired eyes, and looked out to the uninterrupted view of the turquoise ocean, dotted with small boats. Since arriving at his luxury hotel, positioned right at the tip of the Varadero peninsula, he had spent almost every waking moment tapping away at the computer keys like a man possessed, breaking from his writing only long enough to walk to the restaurant and back at meal times. He didn't like Varadero much, apart from the amazing view, it was far too commercial for his taste and lacking any authentic Cuban character, but it was serving his purpose well. Since arriving, three days previously, he had written twenty thousand words of his new novel. Having suffered such a writer's block on his second book, he couldn't quite believe how easily it was all flowing. It helped having no distractions. He had emailed Jo the moment he arrived in Varadero:

Jo,

My next book is plotted. I'm about to start writing and I don't want any interruptions, so don't bother emailing me because I won't be checking them and my phone is now off!

With a bit of luck, you should have a first draft in two weeks. I've always been good with deadlines

Phil

He had no idea if Jo had responded as he had stuck to his guns and not looked at his emails and, true to his word, his mobile phone was zipped away in a pocket in his suitcase. Out of sight, out of mind, he thought. If I can't see the phone, I won't be tempted to turn it on and check for non-existent calls from Holly.

Havana had initially seemed a disastrous choice of destination with the heat, the noise and noxious smell of petrol fumes but, on his first morning, having resisted the temptation of the minibar in his hotel room, Philippe had gone exploring. As he'd walked along cobbled streets, lined on either side by centuries-old, pastel-painted buildings, whose wrought-iron balconies overhung the bustling streets below, the seed of an idea for his next novel started to germinate in his brain.

As a former journalist, Philippe was never without a notepad and pen, and by the time he had finished his second bottle of the locally brewed Tinima beer, sitting outside a bar frequented by locals rather than tourists, his notebook was full of scribbled ideas. The physical features of the characters were all based on real people who had passed the small round table he was sitting at and the minor everyday dramas became the side stories in his plot. He had watched from his vantage point as a group of seemingly unconnected locals gathered to help push a bright purple car out of the flow of traffic. Philippe thought it had broken down but fifteen minutes later the driver returned to his car and drove off.

While ordering his third bottle of beer, and a sandwich to soak it up, Philippe asked the barman about what he had observed.

'It's very common here,' the barman had replied. 'If the gearbox breaks on American cars the local mechanics can't get the parts to repair it. They fix it to drive okay going forwards but without reverse gear. If you need to park and the space is not big enough to drive into, you stop in the road by the parking space and wait for people to come and push you.'

Philippe smiled. He couldn't imagine anything similar happening on a busy London street, or anywhere in the developed world for that matter. Cuba was refreshingly different with its lack of fast-food chain outlets and global shopping brands. It had a personality and charm all of its own. It would be sad to see that diluted or, worse still, disappear, if the proposed changes in its relationship with America went ahead.

He slid a few pesos over the bar to pay for his beer and sandwich and headed back to his table. From out of nowhere, a scraggy-looking ginger cat had appeared and was waiting by his red plastic chair. Very savvy, he thought, pulling a few pieces of meat out of his sandwich and dropping them on to the cobbles by his feet. Within moments, one cat had become five. They were all quite thin and unkempt-looking but they shared the meat without fighting among themselves. Minutes later, each one satiated, they dispersed to find their own corner in the sun to sit and clean themselves. Even the stray cats seemed to share the laid-back Cuban attitude to life.

He took another swig of slightly flat beer and continued writing notes. His main character was the hard-nosed, ambitious editor of a publishing company who had surprised all her work colleagues by falling in love with the mild-mannered owner of a bookshop while on holiday in Cuba. She was so besotted with him that she had promptly resigned from her job. Unbeknown to her, the bookshop was really the distribution centre for a drug cartel. Write about what you know with a few embellishments, thought Philippe, unable to resist smirking.

By the time he climbed in a taxi for the drive to Varadero two nights later, he had the whole story plotted and he'd even managed to squeeze in a visit to the Tropicana Cabaret, allegedly the oldest and most famous cabaret show in Cuba. He was glad he had. Not only did it give more local colour in his book, he had also enjoyed taking his mind off the situation with Holly by indulging in a few mojitos and Cuba libres while admiring the lithe acrobats and dancers.

When the first draft of the book is finished and emailed to Ripped, he thought, I'll go back to the UK and resolve the situation with Holly once and for all.

CHAPTER 30

'Thank you for coming,' Holly said, as Harry swung Toby, his green Vauxhall Corsa, into a tight space in the hospital car park.

'That's okay, Mum. This is far too big a situation for you to face on your own and besides, she asked to see me too. I'm glad you decided to come back early from Mexico. I didn't realise that so many long-haul flights come into the regional airports now. It's just as well you didn't take Rosie on this trip.'

'I know. I barely had three days there in the end. I owe Amy for agreeing to look after her while you came up here to be with me. She really is an angel.'

'It's funny you should use that word, Mum, that was what I called her the very first time we met.'

Holly shot her son a sideways glance before releasing her seatbelt and climbing out of the car. Did she detect something in his voice?

'Well, if you realised that three years ago, how on earth did you manage to let her slip through your fingers?'

'I thought she preferred Jack to me,' Harry said, locking the car and linking arms with his mum, 'but I can see now that I didn't really give us a chance. If I'm honest, I think I was a bit scared about falling for the first girl that I'd spoken to at uni. I didn't want to commit to someone and then it be awkward if we split up. I virtually pushed Amy in to Jack's outstretched arms. I know, you don't need to say it, I'm an idiot.'

Even with her mind so full of other things, Holly fervently hoped that her son and Amy would be able to make a go of things, now he had finally seen what had been right under his nose for almost three years. Maybe some good will come of my abortive trip to Mexico after all, she thought.

'Well it's a good job *On The Sofa* had bumped me up to business class. I'm pretty sure that made it much easier to change the flights for a second time. My blog isn't going to be a patch on my usual standard but I simply didn't have time to take the trips I'd planned. I hope Soleil won't sack me.'

'That would be a pretty shitty thing to do under the circumstances. You did explain that your mum was critically ill in hospital and not expected to survive the week, didn't you?'

Holly nodded, her bottom lip quivering.

'I was worried sick that something might happen to her before you got back, so it was great being able to save you the couple of hours driving up from London.'

Holly and Harry had reached the end of a corridor in the Queens's Medical Centre in Nottingham and were checking the sign for directions to the ward that Carol was on.

'This way,' Harry said, steering his mother to the left.

'Thanks for speaking to the carer too, Harry. What did

you say her name is?'

'Helen. She sounds really pleasant but very upset. She obviously cares for your mum a great deal.'

'It's lucky she was living at Mum's house and called the ambulance so promptly, otherwise it doesn't bear thinking about.' Holly stopped abruptly. 'What I don't understand is why she would try to take her own life now? She's lived all these years without trying to contact us and then when she does finally reach out, she doesn't allow time for us to respond. It doesn't make sense.'

'Helen said she wrote the letter when she was having a good day and felt positive about wanting to see you and ask your forgiveness. Apparently, the dementia causes her to have memory loss, time lapses and violent mood swings. Perhaps in her head she thought she'd written to you ages ago and when you hadn't replied she couldn't see the point of carrying on living.'

'Do you think she'll know who I am, Harry?'

'I honestly don't know, Mum, but in a way it's not important. More important is that you're here, regardless of the way she has treated you over the years. You found it in your heart to forgive her.'

'She's still my mum and your grandma, Harry,' Holly said, approaching the nurse's station. 'We're all she's got and, whatever she's done in the past, it's never too late to say you're sorry. Excuse me,' she said, addressing the nurse, 'we're here to see Carol Wilson.'

'Oh yes, you must be Carol's other daughter,' the nurse said. 'Helen told us you were on your way. It's out of visiting times but the doctor said it would be all right under the circumstances. This way. She's in a room on her own so that Helen could stay with her round the clock.'

Holly must have misheard. She could have sworn the nurse said 'other' daughter.

'What did she just say?' Holly whispered, as the nurse led them towards a door at the far end of the ward.

Harry shrugged.

'I'm sure she said "other" daughter. What does she mean?'

'Maybe they assumed Helen is related to Carol because she came in with her.'

Holly was still looking puzzled as the nurse pushed the door open and let them pass before closing it behind them to give them privacy. The grey-haired woman sat at Carol's bedside jolted upright.

'Oh, I'm sorry, I must have dozed off. I'm Helen,' she said, releasing Carol's hand so that she could shake Holly's.

'I'm Holly and this is my son Harry, who you've been talking to on the phone. How is she?'

'Pretty much the same. The doctors have kept her heavily sedated since the first time she came round. She was screaming and shouting and trying to pull the tubes out of her arms. That's why they put us in here. She was scaring the other patients.'

'The nurse said it was so you could stay with her twenty-four seven,' Holly said, approaching the bed, her eyes gradually adjusting to the dimness of the room.

'Well, yes, that too. I didn't want her to come round and not know where she was so I've stayed with her since she was admitted.'

'Thank you for taking such good care of Mum, we're very grateful. Do you want to have a break? Maybe go back to the house and get some fresh clothes? We're here now. We'll look after her if she wakes up.'

'I'd rather not, if it's all right with you. I'd never forgive myself if something happened to her and I wasn't here.'

'Why do you care so much, Helen?'

The older woman's gaze dropped down to her hands.

'Is it because she is more than just your patient?' Holly said, her pulse quickening.

'Mum,' Harry said, resting his hand lightly on her shoulder. 'I'm not sure this is the time or place.'

'The nurse told you, didn't she? I asked her not to but I guess she forgot. Not surprising really, they're run off their feet. I didn't want you to find out like this,' she said, bringing her eyes up to meet Holly's, 'but, yes, I'm your sister, well, half-sister to be more accurate.'

'I-I don't understand. Are you claiming that Mum is your mum too? How? She never mentioned having any other children. Neither did my dad for that matter and he would never keep secrets from me. You're surely not suggesting that my dad didn't know either?'

'It happened quite some time before Carol met your dad,' Helen said, carefully.

'But that's impossible. Mum met Dad when she was only sixteen, they were married when she was eighteen and I was born a year later. There must be some mistake. How do I know you're telling the truth?'

'What would I possibly gain by lying to you? I didn't know until a couple of years ago that Carol was my birth mother and by that time she was already suffering from dementia. As a trained nurse, I was able to take an additional qualification before applying to be her live-in carer. They were contemplating putting her in an institution.'

'So you tracked her down out of the kindness of your heart after all these years, even though she'd given you up for adoption?' Holly was remembering the conversation she had so recently had with Nick, where he had shown no such interest in the whereabouts of his birth mother.

'It was a little more selfish than that. I wanted to know who my father was, and find out why she gave me away,' Helen said, her voice trembling.

'And did you?'

'Yes, but in some ways I wish I hadn't. No wonder she turned to drink. There is a lot in her past that she wanted to forget,' Helen said, a pained expression on her face.

Holly had read the note that Helen had sent to her along with Carol's letter. 'What aren't you telling me?'

'I'm not sure you're ready to hear the full story. This has all been quite a shock for you and you must be exhausted after your long flight.'

'Tell me,' Holly said, the volume of her voice rising.

'Shhh, Mum,' Harry said, taking hold of her hand, 'remember where we are.'

'You're right, Harry,' Holly said, breathing deeply to regain control of her emotions. 'So, how did Mum react when her long-lost daughter appeared out of the blue? Presumably she checked to see you are who you say you are?'

'She doesn't know,' Helen said, her voice a barely audible whisper.

'What do you mean, she doesn't know? Why on earth wouldn't you tell her?'

'Dementia is a complicated illness. Not only do sufferers get easily confused, they can also block out entire passages of their life that were traumatic. I wanted Carol to trust me so that she would tell me what had happened in her past. I was afraid that if I told her I was the baby she had given up for adoption, her defence mechanism would kick in and then I would never discover the truth.'

'But you said a few moments ago that she has told you who your father is, so why haven't you revealed who you are to her?'

'I was going to. I was looking for the right moment and searching for the right words and then you turned up on her TV screen. I could see she was battling with herself, wanting to still hate you, because she blamed you for causing your dad's death, but at the same time wanting to love you and beg for your forgiveness. Telling her about me would have pushed her completely over the edge. I thought we had a bit more time but now, with this overdose...' her voice trailed off.

The two women fell silent, both staring at the frail woman on the hospital bed that neither had been able to enjoy a normal mother-and-daughter relationship with.

'I'm sorry for doubting you,' Holly said, reaching her hand out towards Helen across the bed. 'You're right; I am in shock. First with Mum contacting me, after vowing she would never speak to me again, and then to find out I have a half-sister... it's all vaguely surreal. How old are you Helen, if you don't mind me asking?'

'I'm forty-six.'

'But that can't be right. Mum turns sixty this coming Christmas; how could she have a child of forty-six, unless she's been lying about her age?'

Helen shook her head slowly. 'No, that's something she hasn't lied about. She was just thirteen when she gave birth to me.'

Holly gasped.

'It gets worse, I'm afraid. I had thought that maybe your mum, I mean, our mum, had fallen in love with someone a lot older than her and had lied to him about her age. I had imagined that when she revealed the pregnancy to her family, the decision to have me adopted had been made with Mum's well-being in mind. It wasn't.' Helen paused, clearly struggling with what she was about to reveal. 'It was to cover up the disgusting actions of our uncle George.'

'Oh my God,' Harry said.

The bitter taste of bile rose in Holly's mouth. 'Are you telling me that Mum was the victim of child abuse?'

Helen nodded. 'Our grandmother had turned to her brother in desperation, after her husband died, and in payment he took our mother's innocence.' Helen was not given to shows of emotion but as she spoke a sob caught in her throat. 'Like I said, I wish I'd left things alone. I'd rather have gone to my grave not knowing that my father was a rapist. It makes me sick to my stomach.'

Holly moved around the bed and pulled her sister into a hug, holding her until the tears subsided.

'If you had left things alone, as you put it, our mother would most probably already be dead. As it is, you've been able to spend time with her, caring for her and getting to know her, and you've probably given her some of the happiest moments of her tragic life. I'm just so sad that she didn't feel able to share some of this terrible guilt she's carried with her all her life with me or my dad. If we'd known, we could have got help for her and she may never have started drinking. What a dreadful waste. What a depraved man; I hope he rots in hell. Uncle George didn't just steal her childhood he ruined her entire life. I can see now why she reacted how she did when I told her I was pregnant with Harry. It didn't matter that I truly loved his dad and that we would probably have got married, all she could see was that, like her, I was damaged goods.'

'Mum,' Harry said, a sense of urgency in his voice, 'she's awake.'

Holly wondered how much of her speech her mother had heard.

'Holly,' Carol said, in a thin reedy voice, 'is that really you?'

'I'm here, Mum,' Holly said, leaning in closer so that her mother could see her, the years and angry words between them falling away like silk from the unveiling of a statue. 'I've missed you.'

'I've missed you too. Your dad always said I was too hasty sending you away. He was right. I'm sorry. You made a mistake, but without mistakes none of us learn anything. Did you bring the boy?' she asked, the effort of talking almost overwhelming her.

Holly beckoned to Harry. 'Yes, Mum, he's here. This is your grandson, Harry,' Holly said, with more than a hint of maternal pride.

'That's not the name we gave him,' Carol said, frowning. 'I think it was Richard, or maybe Nicholas, but they took him away from me. They wouldn't let me keep him, just like the first time.'

Holly, Helen and Harry exchanged glances.

'Do you know what she's talking about?' Holly mouthed to Helen.

'I've no idea,' Helen whispered back. 'She gets confused like this sometimes but I've never heard her mention those names before.'

'Is that you, Helen? You see, I told you Liberty Sands was my daughter. She's beautiful isn't she? She looks just like my Will. He's waiting for me. I think he's got the baby,' Carol's eyes were closing again.

'You get some rest, Carol. We'll be here when you wake up,' Helen said soothingly.

'Did I tell you I'm sorry, Holly?' she mumbled, slipping back into a drug-induced sleep.

'Yes, Mum,' Holly reassured her, tears falling from the tip of her nose, but Carol could no longer hear her.

CHAPTER 31

Amy heard the phone ringing as she slipped her key into the front door lock. Rosie, usually so good-natured, had been uncharacteristically fractious after her lunch, so Amy had decided to take her for a walk. The movement of the buggy lulled Rosie to sleep fairly quickly but Amy had stayed out anyway, enjoying the feeling of the spring sunshine on her face and bare arms. The past two days had been a delicious blur for Amy since confessing her love to Harry. The two of them had always been close as friends but now there was an intimacy between them that only lovers shared.

Following the discovery of Carol's letter and the subsequent Facetime call with Holly, the two of them had spent the rest of the day doing mundane domestic chores and taking care of baby Rosie. Harry had come downstairs after putting Rosie to bed that evening, crossed to the sofa where Amy was sitting reading a book and pulled her into an embrace, kissing her passionately until they had both been gasping for air.

'I always wondered what you would taste like,' Harry said.

'Well, it's a good job you didn't wait until after dinner to do that or it would have been garlic bread,' Amy joked.

'I like garlic bread,' Harry said, pulling her face towards him and kissing her again.

Amy had never experienced the sensations she was feeling and they were only kissing. Sex with Jack had been energetic and physically satisfying, particularly in the early days of their relationship, but she had always felt there was something missing. Now she knew what that was. She had never truly loved Jack with all her heart. She could feel Harry's desire through his clothes but abruptly he pulled away from her.

'I have to stop now Amy. I want you with every inch of my body but it wouldn't seem right in my mum's bed and here on the sofa makes me feel like a naughty teenager. Are you okay to wait until we are back in Bath? I want our first time to be perfect.'

Amy smiled. She was certain that making love with Harry would be perfect wherever they were, but he needed to feel comfortable too.

'I've waited this long,' she said, 'another couple of days won't kill me.'

As she dragged the buggy over the front door step, attempting not to jostle Rosie to the point of waking her up, she wasn't so sure. All she could think about was the feel of Harry's lean body next to hers and the touch of his fingers bringing her pleasure. The phone, which had stopped ringing while she struggled with the double lock, started up again, startling her out of her reverie.

She snatched it up on the second ring hoping she had caught it before it disturbed Rosie.

'Hello,' she said, as quietly as she thought could feasibly

be heard on the other end of the phone.

It was Harry.

'She's gone, Amy.'

Amy was confused for a moment. Harry sounded weird. He must have somehow have managed to miss meeting up with his mum at East Midlands airport.

'Perhaps your mum got a taxi straight to the hospital?' she suggested.

'I don't mean my mum,' Harry said. 'I picked her up from the airport as arranged. My grandmother just died.'

'Oh my God, Harry, I'm so sorry. Did you and Holly get to see her before... I mean, in time?'

There was a pause. Harry was nodding on the other end of the phone line, not trusting himself to speak, but Amy couldn't see him.

'Are you okay?' she ventured.

'Not really. I've never seen a dead person before. One minute she was talking to Mum and then she just closed her eyes as though she was sleeping. And then the machine monitoring her heart stopped beeping and started making a continuous noise, just like you see on *Casualty*. The nurses rushed in and made us wait outside her room but there was nothing they could do. It was almost as though she had held on just long enough to see Mum.'

'And you, Harry.'

'She didn't know who I was. She was completely lucid one minute and the next she was talking about Mum's dad Will, coming to see her with a baby.'

Amy could feel Harry's hurt. After a lifetime of his grandmother ignoring his existence, she had finally asked to meet him. It had taken a lot of courage for him to accompany his mum to the hospital and in the end it had been for nothing. According to Harry, she hadn't even realised he was there.

'I don't really know what to say. I'm sorry it didn't work out as you'd hoped. Are you and your mum still at the hospital?'

'No. We're at my grandma's house with Helen. Everything's such a mess, Amy.'

'I thought Helen was supposed to be looking after her. Hasn't she been doing her job properly?'

'Not the house, that's spotless, I mean the whole situation. It's too complicated to explain over the phone. I'll tell you all about it tomorrow, assuming you'll be okay to look after Rosie overnight? I know I said I'd drive back this evening but I don't want to leave Mum and she won't leave Helen. Will you be able to manage?'

There were so many questions floating around in Amy's head but she would have to wait for the answers.

'Of course. We'll be fine. Tell your mum not to worry and give her a big hug from me.'

'Thank you, Amy, you really are an angel. I said it in fun when we first met but now I know it's true.'

'Let me just adjust my halo,' Amy said.

'I mean it. And there's something else. I should have told you the other day when you told me how you feel …'

Amy's heart was beating wildly.

'I love you too, Amy. I'm sorry it's taken me so long.'

'It's never too late to say how you feel,' she said, aching to be in his arms.

CHAPTER 32

'Are you sure you're okay?' Tamsin asked, deftly twisting a section of Holly's hair around a heated roller and clipping it in place. 'The bottom line is, it's only five minutes of television. I'm sure they could fill it with something else. Let's face it, they'd have to if you had lost your voice.'

Holly made eye contact with her make-up artist through the large mirror framed by light bulbs.

'I'll be fine. Like you said, it's only five minutes and it will give me a sense of normality. I'm just sorry I've given you such a tough job this morning.'

'I enjoy a challenge,' Tamsin replied, smiling.

Holly looked at her own reflection. Gone were the red-rimmed, puffy eyes and dark circles, expertly hidden by Tamsin's skill and professional-grade concealer. She looked exactly the same as she had on her previous appearances on television but she knew she would never feel the same again. *On The Sofa* had reunited Holly and her mother, however briefly, and for that she would be eternally grateful, not least because she was now aware of a sister she didn't know she had. Holly closed her eyes and pictured the small but tidy living room with the same dark green velour couch that she had snuggled up on as a child next to her father, while her mother had sat alone in her armchair. For the hundredth time in the past two days Holly questioned why her mother had felt unable to confide in her and her dad. Things might have been so different, Holly thought, if she had let us help her.

It had been a wrench to leave Helen in Clifton the previous day. Holly had wanted her sister to travel back to Reading with them but realised the impracticality of her suggestion. She only had a two-bedroom house which was already full to bursting with Harry, Amy and baby Rosie, so she had nowhere for Helen to sleep. As they had hugged on the doorstep, Helen assured Holly she would rather keep busy sorting out their mother's things and making arrangements for the funeral.

Helen would also have to meet with her employers. Carol had taken a near fatal overdose while in her care and although there was unlikely to be any blame attributed to her there were still questions to be answered. She had told Holly there were some questions of her own she wanted answering, primarily, where had Carol got the whisky from? The two of them had discovered her hiding place behind the water cylinder in the airing cupboard in the bathroom, but who had provided it? It was something they needed to get to the bottom of.

'Let's do your lipstick and then we'll get these rollers out. You're so lucky with your hair, Holly. Most people need half an hour and half a can of hairspray to achieve the volume you have, whereas you need five minutes to tease your curls into a more telly-friendly style.'

Holly presented her lips for their application of

'passionfruit pink' lip gloss, appreciative of Tamsin's attempt at normal conversation.

'Beautiful,' Tamsin said, a few minutes later, standing back to admire her handiwork, 'go and knock 'em dead. Oh gosh, sorry,' she said, realising too late her inappropriate choice of words.

'It's okay,' Holly said, handing over the peach make-up cape that had been protecting her emerald green dress from any spills, 'it's an easy slip of the tongue.'

Holly went in search of her mic and talkback unit. It was usually the production assistant's job to mic her up but she hadn't seen Maddie that morning.

'Hi Tom,' she said to the sound man, 'no Maddie this morning?'

'She's in the gallery, sitting in for Richard. Apparently, he's been summoned upstairs by the big brass,' he added, raising his eyebrows speculatively. 'Are you okay if I unzip your dress to clip these on your bra strap?'

'That would sound so wrong coming from anyone but a sound engineer,' Holly said, turning her back to Tom. 'Go for it.'

'Best job in television,' smiled Tom, without sounding in the least bit sleazy.

Fifteen minutes later the Liberty Sand's travel slot was over for another week and Holly had to disagree with Tom's previous comment. Surely I have the best job in television, she thought, as he removed the packs from her bra strap.

'Maddie asked me to pass on that you need to hang around until the end of the show. Everyone's got to attend a meeting in the production office. She apologised under the circumstances. Sorry about your mum by the way, I didn't want to say anything before you went on air in case it upset you.'

'Thanks, Tom. Any idea what's going on?'

'Not a Scooby but we'll all find out soon enough, I guess.'

'Okay, okay, settle down,' Richard said, calming the room with his hand gesture. 'As I was saying, because of the executive producer's alleged impropriety, which was brought to the board's attention by a whistle-blower who wishes to remain anonymous, there will be some changes but they won't affect most of you. Your jobs are safe, unless of course you decide to leak anything to the press, in which case you would face instant dismissal. I hope I've made myself clear? All the personnel changes will take effect immediately. Thanks for your cooperation and have a good weekend. Maddie and Holly, can I have a couple more minutes please? Let's go into my office.'

'Congratulations,' Holly muttered, as the two of them crossed the production office.

'Likewise,' Maddie said, winking.

'What do you mean?'

'All will be revealed,' she said, holding the door open for Holly and closing it behind them.

'Right, well I'll get straight to the point,' Richard said. 'It's largely thanks to you two that I've been promoted to replace our disgraced executive producer – every cloud and all that. Maddie, you found Holly and could see the potential in her, which persuaded me to give her a chance. That's why I recommended you as my replacement for *On The Sofa*. It's a huge step up, so don't let me down.'

'I appreciate the opportunity, Richard, and I won't disappoint you.'

'Good. As for you Holly, your probationary period with us is terminated.'

Holly gasped. She could feel the floor slipping away from under her. She had tried her hardest to do everything they had asked of her, even agreeing to cut short her Soleil trip at the risk of losing her other employment. Two pairs of eyes looked at her expectantly.

'I'm sorry. What did you say?'

Richard raised his eyebrows skywards. 'I said, it gives me great pleasure to offer you a two-year contract, terms to be negotiated with your agent. Congratulations. I know this hasn't been the best week for you, but hopefully it's ended on a more positive note. And, Holly, well done for this morning, it can't have been easy. We were all watching you upstairs and everyone agreed we've found a gem in you.'

Holly made it out of Richard's office before the tears started to roll. Maddie put her arm around her and guided her towards the ladies' room.

'It's okay,' she said, 'let it all out. You'll feel better for it.'

After a few minutes Holly's tears subsided.

'I don't know how to feel,' she said. 'It feels wrong to be happy when I've just lost my mum and the executive producer has just lost his job.'

'I'm sorry about your mum, Holly, but don't waste your pity on the exec. producer. He had it coming, the dirty old sod!'

In that moment, Holly knew who had blown the whistle on the executive producer but why was Maddie letting her in on the secret when she clearly wanted to hide it from everyone else?

'I'm going all the way to the top, Holly. Stay on side and I'll take you with me, but cross me and you'll disappear before the ink is dry on your contract. Here,' she said, handing Holly a paper towel, 'your mascara's smudged.'

CHAPTER 33

Although Holly was eternally grateful to Amy and Harry for staying at her home in Reading and taking care of Rosie, she had to admit she was a little relieved to wave them goodbye on Saturday morning. It was great to see the pair of them so loved-up, but it made her situation with Philippe seem even more impossible. Of course, she and Philippe were older, and they had Rosie as an added complication, but Holly had to question again whether he was the right man for her. She still fancied him like mad, and missed him when they weren't together, but she wasn't totally bereft when they were apart. And then there was the trust issue. Philippe had made no attempt to flirt with Maddie and yet she had immediately suspected them of a clandestine meeting merely because they had both been in Dublin at the same time. How ridiculous am I? she thought, shifting Rosie on to her hip and reaching for the vacuum cleaner from the understairs cupboard.

'No wonder your daddy is ignoring my texts and calls, he's probably reached the conclusion that I'm not worth the effort,' she said to Rosie, who was stretching her chubby little hand up trying to reach the sparkly stud earring in Holly's ear.

Holly had been trying to reach Philippe since her mother's death on Wednesday evening. Although he had never met her mother, Holly felt as though she needed someone to lean on apart from her son, who was mourning the lost opportunity of trying to build a relationship with his estranged grandmother. She had resisted the urge to ring Gareth. Since his declaration of love for her she had reached the conclusion that the only way to be fair to him was to maintain a friendship from a distance. She was hopeful he would eventually appreciate the depth of Megan's feelings for him and reciprocate them.

'Looks like it will just be me and you, princess. I hope you'll be okay with that,' Holly said, pushing the vacuum cleaner forward and backwards in rhythmic strokes, leaving a striped effect on the carpet, not dissimilar to the grass on Centre Court on the first day of the Wimbledon tennis tournament.

Vacuuming finished, Holly headed upstairs to strip the sheets off the beds. She needed to keep busy with household chores to stop her from thinking about the events of a traumatic couple of weeks. Once the sheets were in the machine, she wheeled Rosie's buggy into the back garden, put the parasol up to protect the baby from the bright sunshine, and fastened the play centre across the front to keep her amused. Rosie loved the row of brightly coloured plastic animals spread along a bungee cord. They seemed to dance every time she touched them with her hands or kicked them with her feet, causing her to squeal in delight.

Confident that the little girl would be happily amused

for thirty minutes or so, Holly dragged the hover mower out of her cramped garden shed and plugged it in to the extension lead. Time for the first mow of the summer, she thought, twisting her hair up into a ponytail with the black elastic band that resided almost permanently around her wrist. It was only a small patch of grass but it was still hot, thirsty work, and a dribble of sweat rolled down her neck and over her collarbone as she went into the kitchen to fetch herself a glass of water. The washing machine had reached its spin cycle, but over the din Holly thought she heard a knock at the front door.

'Mummy won't be a minute, Rosie,' Holly called to her daughter, as she headed for the front door. Rosie, still totally engrossed in her game, was oblivious to the remark.

'Robert,' Holly exclaimed, 'what a lovely surprise. I hope you haven't been standing out here long. I was in the garden mowing the lawn and I've got the washing machine on too.'

'We just arrived this minute.'

'We?' Holly asked, suddenly feeling self-conscious about her appearance.

'Yes, Nick drove me over. The Jag had a puncture and I didn't want to let you down after promising Harry I'd pop over and make sure you were okay. He did tell you I was coming, didn't he?'

'Yes, of course,' Holly lied, 'but I thought he said this afternoon. I was just doing a bit of tidying up in readiness. Hi, Nick,' she added, colouring up in embarrassment at the thought of him seeing her in such a dishevelled state, as he came into view over Robert's shoulder. 'Come in.'

'Not me,' Nick said, 'I'm just the chauffeur. I'll have

a walk into town or something and pick you up around four, Robert.'

'Don't be silly,' Holly said. 'You'll have to excuse the mess because I've only just got around to spring cleaning but, if you can put up with that, you're both very welcome.'

'There you are, Nick,' Robert said, leading the way into the house. 'I told you Holly would be fine with you staying. Rosie, where are you darling?' he called, leaving the two of them on the doorstep.

'Well, if you're sure you don't mind. I'll try not to get under your feet. I quite like cleaning, as it happens, so I'll give you a hand if you like. Do you want me to help you with the windows? They're looking a bit grubby. Sorry, I didn't mean it like that,' he said, instantly colouring up.

'No offence taken,' Holly said, smiling. 'I'll probably run out of energy or time or both before I attempt those. I'd forgotten how time-consuming bringing up a baby is. Loads of little jobs get left in preference to caring for Rosie.'

'Which is how it should be. You can never get precious moments like first smiles and first words back, but dirty windows will always be there.'

'So they've turned from grubby to dirty in the space of two minutes,' Holly teased. 'Maybe I should take you up on your offer of cleaning them or I won't be able to see out of them at all by the end of the day. Can I get you a drink? Coffee, tea or maybe a cold drink?'

'Tea would be lovely. I'm not that fond of coffee. One cup in the morning is usually my limit. I like the taste of it but I don't like the smell it leaves on my breath.'

Holly led him through to the kitchen, trying to remember if she had brushed her teeth after breakfast, before starting on the housework. She kept her face averted from his while she prepared tea for him and Robert, then excused herself for a few minutes, rushing up to the bathroom to brush them, just in case. By the time she came downstairs, five minutes later, Nick was winding up the cord on the mower, having finished the job for her.

'You didn't need to do that,' she said.

'I thought I should try to make amends for the comment about the windows.'

'You haven't been upsetting our host, have you, Nick?' Robert joked.

'Of course he hasn't,' Holly said, smiling appreciatively. 'Would you be able to put the rotary dryer up for me while I get the sheets out of the machine? They should be dry in next to no time in this sunshine.'

'Yes ma'am,' Nick said, bowing his head slightly and touching his forehead with his hand as though he were a servant from the Victorian era.

Holly retreated to the kitchen feeling oddly exhilarated. When she emerged a few moments later carrying a white plastic basket full of wet bed linen, Robert was lifting Rosie out of her buggy.

'She's bored in there, bless her,' he said, sitting back down on one of the garden chairs.

'You spoil her, Robert,' Holly said, crossing the short distance to the clothes airer.

'That's not true, is it, princess?' he said, supporting Rosie under her arms while she made the effort to stand on his thighs, her toes curled under, preventing her feet from flattening out. 'She's got such strong legs. What age are they supposed to start walking?'

'They're all different. Harry was on his feet before his first birthday but I think that was quite early. What age did your twins walk, Nick?'

'I can't really remember. Round about their first birthday too, I think. I wish I'd realised back then that they were going to be my only offspring. I would have paid more attention to each little miracle of their growing up. That's the problem with being a young parent, I didn't fully appreciate how special each new thing they did was. I'm sure I'd make a very different parent now.'

'Well, it's not too late to have more children, Nick. You're not even forty yet. Some men of my age become fathers for the first time.'

'There's a slight flaw with that plan, Robert, I don't have a wife any more.'

'There's plenty more fish in the sea, Nick, especially for someone as handsome as you who earns a pretty penny. Isn't that right, Holly?'

Holly was grateful that she had her back to the pair of them as she struggled not only with the king-size duvet cover, but also the blush that was creeping across her cheeks. 'Mmmm,' was all she could muster in response.

Not prepared to let it drop, Robert said, 'You should get yourself on one of those dating websites. You'd have women queuing up to go on a date with you.'

'Not my thing at all, Robert. I prefer to meet women the old-fashioned way.'

'Well it's not working very well at the moment, is it?'

'Robert!' Holly exclaimed. 'Nick's divorce has only just come through. Give him a break.'

'It's all right, I'm used to Robert's bluntness. When I'm ready to ask someone out, Robert, you will be the second person to know,' Nick said, skilfully diffusing the potentially awkward situation.

Holly made a ploughman's type lunch from the groceries that Amy had thoughtfully got in for her, with French bread, cheese, ham, pickle and coleslaw, which they enjoyed in the back garden. None of them had noticed the gathering clouds while they had been eating, so the first drops of rain were a surprise.

'You take the plates, Holly. I'll get the sheets and you take Rosie, Robert,' Nick said, immediately springing into action.

Within moments the sky had darkened to a deep grey and the drops of rain had turned into a downpour. Nick had been out of the blocks like a greyhound, but he hadn't been quick enough to prevent the washing from getting damp.

'Do you want these in the tumble dryer?' Nick asked, his eyes scanning the kitchen.

'I haven't got one,' Holly admitted. 'I've always thought they would be too expensive to run. I might just treat myself now that I've been offered a proper contract with *On The Sofa*.'

'You've kept that quiet,' Robert said, slightly aggrieved.

'I only found out yesterday. There was a very high-level firing and, as a result, Richard was promoted to an executive role, Maddie is now the producer of *On The Sofa* and I've been offered a two-year contract.'

'That's fantastic news. It makes up for your dreadful start to the week.'

'Well, I wouldn't exactly say that, Robert, but at least it

means I won't have to worry about money so much any more.'

Holly noticed the exasperated look that Nick shot in Robert's direction, but the man himself was seemingly oblivious.

'Congratulations. I hope it all works out for you. I must admit I was surprised when Robert flicked the television on yesterday and there you were. It was very brave of you.'

'Not really. My mum and I weren't close so it seems a little hypocritical to be devastated by her death. Don't get me wrong, I'm really sad that she's gone, but I'm much more upset about finding out the reason that she became the person she was. What a tragic waste of a life, particularly missing out on all the joy that Harry would have brought her. But some good has come of it all. Did Robert tell you I've discovered a sister that I knew nothing about? She was adopted, like you, Nick,' Holly said, a challenging note in her voice.

'Yes. And look what she found when she tracked her birth mother down. That's precisely why I have no intention of doing it myself,' Nick countered, holding her eyes in a steady gaze.

'But if she hadn't,' Holly persisted, 'my mum and I would never have been reconciled and I still wouldn't know of my sister's existence.'

'True,' he acquiesced. 'Do you think you'll stay in touch after the funeral? When is it by the way?'

'It's a week on Monday. I'm going up to Nottingham on Tuesday to help Helen with the arrangements. I would have gone on Monday, but I've arranged to have lunch with Jo from Ripped Publishing. I don't want to cancel because she'll think I'm making excuses not to meet up with her and I don't want to get on her bad side again. If anything goes wrong with *On The Sofa* or Soleil I need to have a backup plan. Not only that, I'd quite like to write a book myself one day and it would be handy if I already had an "in" with Ripped.'

'I didn't realise you harboured a secret desire to write a book,' Robert said. 'I'm not sure how Philippe would feel about two novelists in the family.'

'It's really not up to him to decide what I can and can't do,' Holly bristled. 'Harry bought me a place on a writer's retreat in Italy for my birthday last year, but I had to postpone going because of my pregnancy. I've been thinking about doing the course in July, when *On The Sofa* is on its summer break and Harry will have finished uni. He and Amy have volunteered to have Rosie,' she added quickly before Robert could volunteer his services.

'I think it's a great idea,' Nick encouraged. 'You've clearly got a talent for writing.'

'How do you know?' Holly asked.

'Well, erm, I've read a couple of your blogs,' he answered, blushing furiously.

Holly coloured up too. What was Nick doing reading her Liberty Sands blog? 'Oh right. Well, I'm glad you enjoyed them. Anyway, to answer your other question,' she said, anxious to change the subject, 'I'll definitely stay in touch with Helen. She seems like a lovely woman and she's got no other family. I'm thinking of inviting her to come and stay with me here for a while when the council take back our mum's house. She's got nowhere else to go.'

'Don't be too hasty, Holly,' Robert said. 'You don't really know much about her.'

'I know you're only looking out for me, Robert, but

you haven't met her. I think you'll like her when you do. Who fancies a cup of tea? I think Amy bought some chocolate digestives.'

'Now you're talking,' Robert said, smiling, but the concern hadn't left his eyes.

CHAPTER 34

There was already a steady hum of conversation from the lunchtime diners in Langan's restaurant as Holly stood at the entrance waiting to be shown to the table Jo had booked.

'I'm so sorry to keep you waiting,' the manager apologised, 'but we weren't advised you would need a high chair. We're sorting that out for you now. Here let me help you.'

'It's okay, I can manage,' Holly said, unclipping Rosie from her safety harness, lifting her on to her hip and deftly collapsing the baby buggy with her foot. 'I hope it's not too much of an inconvenience. My lunch companion should have mentioned it when she made the reservation,' she continued, smiling disarmingly at the manager.

'It's no trouble at all. We enjoy having children in the restaurant. Let me know if there is anything special she would like that isn't on the menu.'

'Rosie will just have a little of my lunch but it would be really helpful if you could warm her bottle. I don't like giving it to her cold unless I have to.'

'You let the waiter know when she's ready and we'll

sort that out for you. This way, I think your table is ready now.'

Holly followed the manager as he negotiated his way through the tables towards the back of the restaurant. She noticed one or two anxious glances from people who were clearly hoping their lunch wasn't going to be disturbed by a screaming infant. She felt smug in the knowledge that Rosie didn't do screaming.

'Oh,' said a voice from behind her, as she fastened the high chair's restraint around Rosie's waist, 'I hadn't realised you were bringing the baby.'

Jo, looking as immaculate as ever in a tailored designer suit with her coppery hair perfectly blow-dried, was unable to disguise the look of displeasure on her face.

'Don't worry, Jo,' Holly said, smiling, 'Rosie really is the perfect baby. So long as she has something to keep her amused,' she indicated the colourful rings she was currently stacking on a sturdy pole, 'you'll barely know she's here.'

'She's a pretty little thing,' Jo said, begrudgingly. 'Your features and Philippe's colouring are a charming combination.'

'My second child and still no sign of my dark curls. It's funny, she looks a lot like her brother did at that age. When people see them together, I'm sure they assume Harry is her father. I should probably have told you I was bringing her along. Sorry. It might be best to order quite quickly. There is a limit to her angelic behaviour.'

'That's fine with me. I'll have my usual. Do you like fish, Holly? If so, I can definitely recommend the rainbow trout.'

'I'd prefer chicken, then Rosie can have some. What

would you suggest?' she asked, turning to the waiter.

Once the food order had been placed, Holly sat back expectantly in her seat.

'So, Jo, why am I here? You already apologised over the phone.'

'I don't remember you being so direct, Holly. Philippe's influence must be rubbing off on you.'

'To be honest, I haven't seen that much of him for him to have an influence on me. In fact, I haven't seen or heard from him in over two weeks.' She watched Jo's face intently, trying to detect her reaction. She had expected satisfaction so was taken aback by her next comment.

'I wouldn't worry about it, Holly. He's taken himself off to Cuba to write his next book. I've never known an author like him. One minute, he doesn't seem to have a clue what he is going to write about, and the next he is sending the first twenty thousand words, with a promise of the finished first draft in a couple of weeks. It must be the newspaper man in him. Give him a deadline, or in his case an ultimatum, and suddenly the creative juices flow.'

Holly felt a bizarre sense of relief. She knew from his previous book that he was very uncommunicative when he was writing. Perhaps that was why he hadn't replied to her calls and texts. Maybe he had been so engrossed in his work that he hadn't even turned his phone on. A thought occurred to her. If he was in Cuba, writing, he might not have received the package containing the ring. There was a glimmer of hope that he was unaware of her breaking things off with him.

'When did he go?' Holly asked.

'A couple of weeks ago. He came back from Dublin and was moaning that you seemed to be avoiding his calls. Honestly, he's such a child, doesn't he realise how busy you are looking after his baby and now with this new career in television? Men. They seem to think they are the only ones who are allowed to go AWOL. Anyway, out of the blue, he suddenly said he was leaving the country. To be fair, I had suggested it during a heated discussion in my office, but I was gobsmacked when he actually said he was going. I'm surprised he didn't let you know. That's just plain rude.'

'No matter,' Holly said. 'He obviously had a sudden flash of inspiration for book three and couldn't wait to get started.'

'Indeed. And it seems I was part of that inspiration,' Jo said. 'I've had the first twenty thousand words and it didn't take me long to recognise myself. Now I know how you must have felt when you started reading *Tiffany*.'

Holly could feel herself blushing. Of course she knew about Jo and Philippe's relationship, which had taken place long before she had met him, but she hadn't realised it had made such an impression on him that he had been inspired to immortalise it in the pages of a book.

'No, not like that,' Jo said. 'There are no tender love scenes involving me and a Philippe-like character. He has painted me as a hard-nosed cow who foolishly falls for a bookshop owner in Cuba who turns out to be a drug dealer.'

'I'm sorry, Jo. I shouldn't laugh, but it is quite funny. How is Geoff by the way?'

'No idea. I think the closest he has ever come to drugs is a paracetamol to help him get over a hangover! Anyway, the point I am making is, now I can empathise with the way you must have felt seeing yourself described in print, but not quite the real you. You know the bit on the title verso page where it says, "any resemblance to any person living or dead is strictly coincidental"? Maybe in Philippe's case it should say "strictly intentional"? I suppose I should be flattered.'

For the first time in a very long time the two women made proper eye contact.

'You know, Holly, I really am terribly sorry about that night at Mosiman's. I let my jealousy of you and Philippe get in the way of any rational behaviour. Can you ever forgive me?'

Holly reached across the table and placed her hand on Jo's arm.

'We go back a long way and I'll always be grateful to you for giving me a chance in the publishing industry. I should have trusted you enough to tell you about my son. I realise now that you judged me by the quality of my work and trusted me with some pretty big manuscripts. If I'd come clean about knowing Philippe, Mosiman's would never have happened. I'm as much to blame as you are.'

'Friends?'

'Friends,' Holly confirmed, 'regardless of what happens between me and Philippe. I'm so glad we've cleared the air, Jo, I've missed you.'

'And I've missed you too. Not least because you are a bloody good copy editor. Some of the people I've had to use over the past few months have fallen so short of your standard.'

'Is that why you wanted to meet? Have you got a juicy manuscript for me? Hold on, you're surely not expecting me to edit Philippe's new book?'

'No, no, it wouldn't be ethical. Actually, it's not a copy

edit. I've an altogether different proposition for you.'

Holly was intrigued but said nothing, concentrating instead on cutting her chicken into bite size pieces for her baby daughter.

'You know I've always encouraged you to write a novel yourself, instead of tidying up other people's work, well, how about writing a travel guide instead? It could be based on your Liberty Sands blogs and now that you've got the *On The Sofa* gig, I reckon we would make a killing. What do you think?'

Holly was actually thinking how weird it was that everything in her professional life was going so well while her private life was falling apart, but she said, 'That's not a bad idea. Who would we get to edit it?'

CHAPTER 35

'Wow, you've been busy. I'm not sure you needed me to come and help. It looks as though you've got everything perfectly under control,' Holly said, casting her eye around her mother's bedroom which was now completely empty apart from the bed and the pretty new curtains at the window.

'I needed to keep occupied, I guess,' Helen replied. 'The obvious place to start was in here. I didn't think you'd want any of Carol's clothes. To be honest, most of them weren't even good enough for the charity shop but those that were, I washed and bagged up. They collected them yesterday morning. There were a couple of coats and dresses she must have had for years that will probably be sold as "vintage" and may raise a few pounds, but the rest will go on the 50p rail.'

Holly was reminded of the many mornings she had spent helping out in her local charity shop while Harry was in infant school. She had always found it incredibly sad when grieving relatives had brought clothes in to be sorted.

'Is that all life amounts to in the end, a pile of shabby,

unwanted clothes?' Holly murmured, her bottom lip quivering.

'You are okay with me giving them to the charity shop, aren't you?' Helen asked. 'I thought I was helping. We could always go and fetch them back if you want. I'm pretty sure they won't have put them out for sale yet.'

'I'm glad you gave them to the charity shop. You'd be surprised what some people buy. We'll probably see a teenager wearing one of the dresses with skinny jeans and trainers, looking like she stepped off the pages of a fashion magazine. I'll be happy if some of the things find a good home. What happened to the rest of the furniture?'

'The wardrobe was falling apart and wouldn't have withstood moving, so I chopped it up for firewood. The next-door neighbour must have heard me and stuck his head over the fence to ask if he could have the chest of drawers for his shed, before it met the same fate.'

'Handy with an axe, are you?' Holly said, unable to resist a smile, as she remembered Robert's words of caution about this person she barely knew.

'I'd never picked one up before I came here. The back garden was in a dreadful state, totally overgrown with brambles, so it was a bonus when I found the little wood axe hiding in a shed that I didn't even know was there, until after I started clearing everything away.'

Holly had a sudden vivid flashback. She and her mum were toasting crumpets, or pikelets as they called them in Nottingham, on toasting forks in front of a roaring fire. Her dad appeared in the doorway, his arms full of logs that he had just chopped, his cheeks pink from the freezing January temperatures. As seven-year-old Holly turned to talk to him, she let the metal fork dip into the flames and moments later she had let out a yelp as the heat travelled up the handle and scalded her hand. She glanced down. The burn mark had long since disappeared but the scar of her mother calling her 'a useless little bitch' had stayed with her for life. She blinked furiously to hold back the tears welling in her eyes.

'What's happening with the bed?' she asked.

'It's no good to anyone. You're supposed to change your mattress every ten years or so but I think this one has lived here as long as Carol did. The council said to leave it and they'll dispose of it when they take the house back.'

'Have you thought what you're going to do, Helen?'

'Oh, I'll get another job easy enough. I'm a trained nurse and now I've got experience as a live-in carer. I'll be fine.'

'Will you stay in Nottingham?'

'I'm not fussed, really. If a decent job comes up then I will, but I wouldn't be averse to a change of scenery. I've always fancied living by the sea. There are plenty of old people's nursing homes dotted around the coast, I could make some enquiries I suppose.'

'Is that what you want?'

'I just want to be happy again. I thought I had the perfect life. A job I loved, a husband I adored who I believed adored me back, but it all crashed down around my ears. I'll tell you about it some time, Holly, just not now. Finding Mum and caring for her, helping her deal with her drink problem, it all gave me a purpose in my life. Now she's been snatched away from me too, without her ever knowing I was her daughter. I try not to feel bitter but sometimes, I confess, it's an uphill struggle.'

'Is it just the elderly you like caring for, Helen?' Holly asked, nonchalantly.

'No, not at all. Anybody who needs me really. I was a paediatric nurse for years. I worked on the premature baby unit. You wouldn't believe the size of some of those little mites who've made their appearance on earth a bit too early. Little miracles they are. Such fighters, clinging on by their non-existent fingernails to their slim chance of survival. Mind you, it's not like it used to be when I first went into nursing. Nowadays, with all the modern technology, most of them have a good chance of making it past the first few crucial hours.'

'It's still a very anxious time for the mother though. My Rosie was two months premature.'

'I didn't know that. Is she all right now?'

'Absolutely fine. She's coming up to seven months and she's already trying to stand,' Holly said proudly.

'Have you got any photos of her?'

'Is that a real question? Come on, let's get ourselves a cup of tea and I'll bore you silly with pictures of her.'

After Holly had exhausted the supply of images of Rosie she had stored on her phone, Helen suggested they continued in a similar vein by looking at the old photo albums she had rescued from the loft a few weeks previously.

'Would you be really offended if I said I'd prefer to take them home with me so that I can pore over them at greater length?' Holly asked.

'No, of course not,' Helen replied. 'It's probably a good idea. Although Carol's room is done, and there isn't much to do in my room, I haven't scratched the surface down here. Do you reckon we can get this room sorted before you have to head back?'

Holly looked around her. There was a floor-to-ceiling bookcase in teak that was spilling its contents like an over-stuffed cushion. Next to that was a matching cupboard, with shelves above it crammed with trinkets and ornaments, most of which Holly or her dad had bought for Carol. On the dining table in front of the window were the photo albums Helen had referred to and a small white document case, which had seen better days.

'It's a tall order, but the sooner we start the sooner we'll finish. What's in the case?'

'I don't know; it's locked. I retrieved it from the loft with the albums, but Carol showed no interest in looking inside. When I asked her about a key for it, she just shrugged her shoulders and said it was your dad's and it was full of his papers.'

'Perhaps we should start with that. She may have left a will.'

'Do you think so? I'm quite an organised person and I haven't made one. Have you?'

Holly shook her head. It was one of those things that she knew she should have done, particularly as a single parent, but she had never got around to it.

'It's the sort of thing my dad would have made her do.'

'How are you going to get into it though? Like I said, it's locked. Should I fetch the axe?'

Holly walked across to the bookcase and picked up an oval shaped brass box. She shook it, and metal rattled against metal.

'I don't think we'll need it. No guarantees, but this was one of Dad's hiding places for stuff. We might be in luck.'

She crossed to the table, pulling the lid off the box on her way and then tipped its contents on to the polished surface. There were several small keys that looked like they belonged to a variety of travel bags and, after trying the first two without success, the third key turned in the lock of the tatty white case. Holly slid the buttons on either side and the T-shaped tabs flew up. Gingerly she raised the lid of the case which she was pretty sure hadn't seen the light of day in twenty years. Holly wasn't sure what she was expecting to find but she had assumed there would be a musty smell. She was pleasantly surprised. The case was neatly packed with bundles of documents but each bundle was individually wrapped in plastic.

'What would you like me to do while you go through that lot?' Helen asked, tactfully.

Holly hesitated. She didn't want Helen to feel as though there was anything in the case that she didn't want her to see, however, Holly had no idea what she was going to unearth.

'You're right, it's pretty pointless us both looking at this stuff,' she said, closing the lid of the case and slipping the key into the pocket of her jeans, grateful that Helen had pre-empted any awkwardness. 'Let's load the albums and the case into the boot of my car and I'll go through them back at home, when I've got a bit more time. Are there any large cardboard boxes? We could make a start by boxing up all the old records. They're no good to me. I haven't got a record player, and I simply haven't got room in my little house to keep any purely for sentimental reasons. Have you got any way of playing them? If you have, you're very welcome to take anything you fancy.'

'I haven't got a turntable either,' Helen said, 'but vinyl is back in fashion, so I'm certain the charity shop will be happy to take these off our hands. What about the books?'

'Books are different. I love old books. Between me and Harry's girlfriend, Amy, we'll probably be able to find a home for most of them.'

Four hours later, they had emptied the bookcase, the cupboard and the shelves. There were three boxes of books stacked by the front door, ready to load into Holly's car for the drive back to Surrey that night. There were also three larger boxes marked CHARITY SHOP, which were full of records and the majority of the ornaments from the shelves, which Holly had agreed should be donated. She had kept a Hummel figurine of a small blond boy fast asleep in a chair, which her dad had helped her chose for her mum one Mothering Sunday. She couldn't recall much about buying it, but the figurine reminded her of a photo of Harry. He had been unusually miserable at the park and Holly had reprimanded him. When they got home he had slumped in an armchair and promptly fallen asleep. The next day his chicken pox rash had appeared, making Holly feel terribly guilty about raising her voice to him.

'Are you sure you want to part with all of this?' Helen asked, a roll of brown parcel tape in her hand in readiness for sealing the boxes.

'Absolutely positive,' Holly responded. 'Hopefully some of those trinkets will bring more pleasure to other people than they ever did our mum. I'm pretty sure she hated stuff like that. I'm only surprised that she kept them all these years.'

'Maybe they meant more to her than you realised,' Helen said.

'You could be right. It just goes to show that, despite living with her for eighteen years, I never really knew her,' Holly said, shaking her head sadly.

'Don't blame yourself, Holly, she wouldn't let you in. Shouldn't you be making tracks if you want to get back to your friend Robert's before Rosie's bedtime?'

Holly glanced at her watch. It was almost four o'clock. The time had run away with them.

'You're right, I should go. It'll take me a good three hours to drive back at this time of day. Is there anything else we need to arrange for the funeral?'

'Nothing, apart from your flowers. It's all pretty low key and the funeral director was very efficient. Did I mention, I put a notice in the Evening Post?'

'I hadn't thought of that. I don't suppose anyone apart from us will turn up to the funeral but you never know.'

'Did you decide whether or not you're bringing Rosie? I'm making some food for us to have here after the cremation. I can get a few bits in for her if you are.'

Until that moment, Holly had been undecided.

'You know, I think I will bring her. Even though she won't understand what is happening and she never met her grandmother, it's a mark of respect for us all to say our goodbyes as a family. And there's no need to worry about food for her, the baby bag is constantly topped up with food, nappies and everything else needed to travel with a seven-month-old baby.'

'I'm pleased you are going to bring her. Apart from

anything else it will give me a chance to have a cuddle with her,' Helen said. 'If that's all right with you of course?' she added.

'I'm sure Rosie will be delighted to meet her auntie Helen,' Holly said, opening the front door before lifting one of the boxes of books to carry to her car, totally missing the tear that escaped from the corner of her sister's eye.

CHAPTER 36

Once again it was Nick, rather than Robert, who was waiting to greet her at the door of Valley View as Holly emerged from her car stretching her limbs, having been cooped up in it for almost five hours.

'You seem to be making a habit of this. Is Robert okay?' Holly asked.

'He's fine,' Nick replied. 'He's just tired. I think he'd underestimated how exhausting it is looking after a young baby for more than a few hours. After he put Rosie to bed he sat on the sofa and five minutes later he was snoring. I sent him to bed.'

'Damn traffic on the M25,' Holly said, following Nick down the sweeping staircase. 'I should have been back two hours ago. I feel dreadful abusing Robert's good nature by being so late. He probably won't volunteer to have Rosie again.'

'You are joking, of course. Rosie is the apple of his eye. She's filled a massive void in his life. He absolutely adores her. Look, I should probably leave you in peace. You must be pretty shattered after your round trip to Nottingham and emotionally drained after sorting through your mum's stuff. There's a chicken casserole in the oven. Hopefully it won't be too dried out.'

'How on earth did Robert find the time to do that as well as caring for Rosie? No wonder he's so worn out. He is such a thoughtful man.'

'Actually, I made it,' Nick said, the familiar flush rising in his cheeks. 'I thought you'd be hungry after your journey and Robert was too preoccupied, so I threw it together for the two of you. As it is, he's gone to bed without eating dinner.'

'Then why don't you stay and have supper with me? It seems a shame to waste good food.'

'I wouldn't judge it until you've tasted it. Like I said, it's probably a bit dried out.'

'In that case, you should definitely have some. Why should I be the only one to suffer?' she teased.

'I guess it beats omelette and microwave chips,' Nick said. 'Do you fancy a glass of wine with it? I put half a bottle of red in the casserole so the other half is going begging. It might help the taste,' he added, a smile playing at the corners of his mouth.

'A glass of red would go down a treat,' Holly said, 'but only if you join me. I don't like drinking alone.'

'Deal. You set the table and I'll dish up.'

Twenty minutes later, Holly kicked off her shoes and sank into the depths of Robert's plush sofa.

'That was really good, not at all dry. In fact, I would go so far as to say it was better than the chicken dish I had for lunch yesterday. Maybe you should have been a chef.'

'I hope you're not doubting my ability as an architect?'

Nick said, settling on the sofa opposite.

'Now you're just fishing for compliments. You know how good you are. Harry is totally in awe of the pair of you.'

'He's a good lad and very talented. You should be proud of him.'

'I am,' Holly said, draining the contents of her wine glass and placing it on the occasional table at her side.

'Refill?'

'No, I'm good thanks. Just nicely relaxed. It wouldn't do for me to fall asleep, snoring, too.'

'It would be a bit of an affront to my ego,' Nick admitted.

'Well, we don't want that, not that you strike me as having much of an ego.'

'Is that a good thing?'

'I would say so. Don't get me wrong, I'm not a fan of false modesty, but I do think it's important to recognise your own ability without pushing it down other people's throats.'

'No wonder Harry is so well adjusted. He's had a great role model in you.'

'Stop it, you'll make me blush.'

'It's funny how we both do that. Does Harry?'

'No. Physically, he's more like his dad. I suppose Rosie is too, really.'

'It's difficult to tell with babies. The twins looked nothing like their mum when they were very young, but I'd say they are much more like her than me now. I think Rosie has a lot of you about her, particularly her mouth and nose. Philippe's nose is very thin if I remember rightly?'

Despite her tiredness, Holly detected a hint of

criticism in Nick's voice. She was pretty sure Nick was not Philippe's biggest fan and couldn't help but wonder what Robert may have said about him during their many hours working together.

'I suppose it is quite Gallic. You make it sound as though you've been studying us. Don't all babies have cute button noses? Not that I think there is anything cute about my nose, it's just kind of ordinary. Is it only ears that keep growing throughout your lifetime or is it noses too?' Holly said, rubbing the tip of hers, distractedly.

'I have no idea. Why are we talking about noses anyway?'

'You started it, but while we're on the subject, I'm so pleased that Harry has finally seen what's right under his.'

'You mean Amy?'

Holly nodded. 'Can you believe it has taken him almost three years to acknowledge he has feelings for her. I hope they can make a go of it. She would be the most perfect daughter-in-law, not that I want them to rush things, of course.'

'Maybe they'll want to make up for lost time. Amy clearly adores Harry and that's my observation after only seeing them together a couple of times. You know when you've met your soulmate, but sometimes it's a case of being patient and waiting until they realise it too.'

'Do you really believe that? I used to think that everyone had just one soulmate, especially having seen Robert and Rosemary and how blissfully happy they were together, but now I'm not so sure. When I met Gareth I was convinced he was the one for me, the person I would spend the rest of my life with, but was it because he was the only love I had ever known? Perhaps I fell in love with him because I was desperate to escape my unhappy childhood. All I do know is that I don't feel the same way about him now, even though there is a small part of me wanting things to be the way they were.'

'None of us can turn back the clock, Holly. You were apart from Gareth for a long time without knowing the reason he didn't come back to you. You couldn't expect to pick things up from where they left off, especially as you now have Philippe in your life.'

There it was again, Holly thought. She couldn't quite put her finger on it, but every time Nick mentioned Philippe's name there was something different about his tone. This time she could have sworn she detected the hint of a question.

CHAPTER 37

Robert closed his bedroom door as quietly as he could, not wanting to alert his two friends, whose conversation he had unintentionally overheard. He padded across the plush carpet, his bare feet sinking into the creamy-white pile, and climbed back into bed, his stomach still grumbling as a consequence of going without his dinner. The aroma of coq au vin had wafted into his bedroom and was partly responsible for waking him up only two hours into his slumber. He suspected he had also been subconsciously listening out for Holly's car tyres on the gravel of the driveway, heralding her safe return. He had been utterly exhausted when he had crawled into bed after a full-on day of looking after baby Rosie, but now he was wide awake.

'Well, Rosie,' he whispered to the heavens, certain that his late wife could hear him, 'what do you make of that?'

Robert had opened his bedroom door just as his houseguests were discussing soulmates. Inevitably they had referenced Robert and Rosemary as the perfect example, and both Holly and Nick had expressed their sorrow at the comparatively short time the Forresters had shared due to meeting each other later in life. Robert, poised to head down to the kitchen to make himself some cheese and crackers, stopped in his tracks. A heavy weight of sadness squeezed his heart and he couldn't trust himself not to break down in front of his friends, so he tiptoed back to his room. It was Holly's remark, as he was about to close the door, that intrigued him and kept him eavesdropping.

After answering Nick's direct question as to whether or not Holly believed Philippe to be her soulmate, she revealed that Philippe had given her an engagement ring for Christmas. Robert was already aware of this after Holly had confided in him during their walk in Battersea Park but the fact that she was sharing her secret with Nick captured his attention. There were a few muffled words that Robert struggled to hear, followed by the admission that she had returned the ring a few weeks previously, believing that Philippe might have been unfaithful to her with Maddie from the television studios.

Robert couldn't be sure but he thought he heard sniffing, as though someone was crying. When the conversation started again it was Nick's voice and it was a little softer. Struggling to hear, Robert crept closer to the bannister.

'Love without trust will never work. If you really want to give things another try with Philippe you will have to trust him completely. It's not fair on either of you, or Rosie, if you don't,' he said gently.

'It's mostly for Rosie that I want to give it a proper chance. She shouldn't have to grow up without a father, like Harry did, because her mother's got trust issues.'

'True, but is giving Rosie what you consider to be a

"normal family life" a good enough reason to get back together if you don't truly love Philippe? There may be someone else, who's perfect for you, waiting just around the corner.'

'I don't know if I can allow myself to fall in love again. My two attempts so far have been pretty disastrous.'

Robert could hear more sniffing and risked a look over the balustrade. Nick had his arms wrapped around Holly and his chin rested on the top of her head.

'You need to open up your eyes and your heart to other possibilities. Your soulmate could be closer than you think,' he said, planting a kiss into her curls. 'It's late. I should go now or I won't be fit for anything in the morning. Did Harry tell you I'm flying out to Hong Kong tomorrow night?' he asked, getting to his feet.

If anything more was said, Robert hadn't heard it as he scuttled back to his room and closed the door.

Lying back on his feather pillows, he continued his conversation with his late wife.

'Nick's talking about himself, Rosie. I've noticed the way he looks at Holly. I think he's been smitten with her since the day he laid eyes on her, but obviously she's been concentrating on trying to work things out with Philippe. I agree with Nick: she's not being fair to anyone if she's only pretending to love Philippe for little Rosie's sake. I wish you were here, my darling. You'd know what to do for the best. I'll have to keep out of it or I'll go and put my foot in things as per usual. I love you, Rosie, and I miss you more than you could ever know,' Robert said, drifting off to sleep, as a tiny curled white feather floated down from his pillow to the floor.

CHAPTER 38

Philippe tapped lightly on the opaque glass door to Jo's office.

'Come in,' she said, without looking up from the papers on her desk. 'I hope you brought me some cigars.'

'I didn't know you smoked them so, no, I haven't, but I did bring you this,' he said, plonking a bottle of white rum in the centre of her papers.

'How the hell have you managed to get so tanned while you've had your head stuck over a computer keyboard every waking hour?' Jo asked, getting to her feet and leaning across her desk to give Philippe the traditional kiss on both cheeks.

'I did allow myself a lunch break, you know. It must have been walking to and from the restaurant and then yesterday I just crashed by the pool. I figured I'd earned it. It's probably to do with my mother's French genes. You redheads never tan easily.'

'I'm not a natural redhead.'

'How could I forget? That was quite a shock when you first stripped off in front of me. Why do you die your hair red?'

'It used to be a power thing, now it's mostly to cover the grey,' Jo confessed. 'You've got a few strands yourself coming through on your temples. On men it's considered sophisticated and experienced, on women it just means we're getting old. There is no such thing as equality.'

Philippe shrugged.

'And you're right, you did earn yourself a day off. Eighty thousand words in three weeks; that must be a record.'

'It's amazing what you can do when you don't have any distractions. Have you forgiven me yet for putting you in the book?'

'Was I in the book?' Jo asked innocently, before throwing her stressbuster ball at him. 'You're a cheeky sod, but at least it's brought Holly and me back together. Now I can empathise with being written about in one of your books. Have you spoken to her since you got back?'

Philippe shook his head.

'So you probably haven't heard that her mother died?'

'No. When? I'm surprised Holly even knows. They haven't spoken for years.'

'Hadn't,' corrected Jo. 'She went to see her in hospital just before she died.'

'Really? That must have been pretty traumatic. They didn't get along at all. Did you know her mum was an alcoholic?'

Jo's eyes flicked over the bottle of white rum.

'I feel like a totally selfish bastard now. I should have been here for a bit of moral support at the very least. When is the funeral?'

'It was yesterday. Haven't you switched your phone on? I'm pretty sure she said she'd been trying to call you when we had lunch together last week.'

Philippe's eyebrows shot up in surprise. 'You had lunch with Holly? What are you up to, Jo?'

'It was business, but I did get to meet your little girl. She was very well behaved, which was a relief considering I took them to Langan's.'

'I can believe Rosie was well behaved but I'm quite surprised Holly didn't scratch your eyes out. On second thoughts, I take that back, Holly wouldn't lower herself to your standards.'

'I probably deserve that. Rest assured, I've apologised unreservedly to Holly and she's accepted. We're going to be working together again.'

'Are you giving her my book to copy edit?'

'You know I can't do that, Philippe, and besides, I'm not sure she's got time to take on any editing work with her new job and the travel blogging.'

'But you said you're going to be working together.'

'We are. I'm just going through her contract now. Holly's joining Ripped on a two-book deal. Don't worry, she's not competing with you. She's going to write two travel books based on her blogs.'

For a moment, Philippe looked stunned.

'Nice move. Sign her up before any other publisher realises just how bankable she is. I've got to hand it to you, Jo, you always were a smart businesswoman.' Philippe cleared his throat. 'I'm glad you've signed Holly, because you're about to lose me.'

Jo's smile faded. 'What?'

'I wanted to tell you in person because without your belief in me I don't think I would have made it as a writer. But you of all people know that business is business. I've been offered a million-dollar advance for my next three books by Parrot Publishers. This latest book is the last one I'll be doing for Ripped.'

'I see,' Jo said, keeping her voice calm. Parrot was one of the biggest publishers in America, and its pockets were very deep. 'Well, I wish you the best of luck. Obviously I'll get our lawyers to look over things and make sure that you haven't breached your contract. We'll get the edits back to you as soon as possible and stick with our planned release in October. I hope Parrot will give you the support we have.'

Jo knew when she was beaten. Ripped couldn't possibly compete with a million-dollar advance. In a way she had expected Philippe to move on after his contracted number of books with Ripped was up, she was however surprised that he had signed with the first big boy to come sniffing around. Jo was pretty sure that he could have doubled his advance in a bidding war. He might be a brilliant writer, she thought, but he has no head for business. It gave her a sliver of satisfaction to know that someone, in an office in one of America's biggest publishing houses, was punching the air at his naivety.

CHAPTER 39

The sky was a bright shade of azure with only a smattering of fluffy white clouds, the sun shone, and the sparrows and blue tits serenaded Holly as she walked through the park, pushing Rosie in her pram. At Carol's funeral the previous day the little girl had behaved impeccably, but the hours in the car had taken their toll. Rosie, who usually kicked her legs excitedly on the way to the park, at the prospect of being pushed on the swings, was asleep before they had reached the end of the road. Holly stayed out anyway, needing the fresh air to clear her head. It had been an emotionally charged day for all of them.

Helen, who had been closest to Carol over the past few months, was visibly distressed as the curtains slid silently back at the crematorium allowing the casket, containing the earthly remains of their mother, to pass through and be engulfed in flames. Holly held her sister's hand tightly to show her support but didn't succumb to tears. She felt desperately sad that her mother had passed away before they had a chance to resolve their issues, but she was also relieved that she had at least been able to see her in her final hours and make some kind of peace. Her certainty that her dad would be waiting for his wife to take care of her in the spirit world, as he had always tried to on earth, brought her enormous comfort.

There had only been the five of them – Holly, Helen, Harry and Amy, and baby Rosie – at the service and mercifully it was brief. Holly couldn't help comparing the funeral with that of Robert's wife, Rosemary, the previous year.

Rosemary had known she was dying and so had been able to plan everything about the ceremony that would celebrate her life. The church was filled with people she loved, who had loved and admired her in return. It was overflowing with flowers and their various fragrant aromas, and the strains of her favourite music floated through the air. There had been plenty of tears shed but, overwhelmingly, the feeling had been one of giving thanks for having known such a special person.

There was very little to celebrate about Carol's life, apart from her being directly responsible for the lives of four of the five people who had gathered to say their goodbyes. She had lost contact with all the friends she had known while her husband had been alive, largely due to her drinking and her unreasonable behaviour. The only people who had featured in Carol's life in her later years were social workers and healthcare professionals. Not even her neighbours, some of whom she had known for more than forty years, felt sufficiently moved by her death to show her the respect of attending her funeral. It was a relief to leave the cavernously empty crematorium building and drive back to the little house in Clifton.

Although Helen had prepared a tasty lunch of quiche,

chicken drumsticks and sandwiches, the sombre mood wasn't lifted until baby Rosie mounted a charm offensive. Having sat quietly on her big brother's knee during the service, she was ready for some action. She was already showing an eagerness to walk and Harry obliged by supporting her under her arms to take the weight off her feet. She 'walked' to each of the adults in turn with Harry's aid and then held on to their legs to support herself, swaying slightly, while she examined the different faces. Most of the time she only managed a few seconds on her feet before sinking down on to her nappy-padded bottom and then reaching her hand out for Harry to repeat the process, a big smile on her face.

'He'll make a wonderful father, one day,' Helen had said to Holly as the two of them tackled the washing-up in the kitchen, while Harry and Amy continued playing with Rosie. 'In fact, they'll make great parents. How long have they been seeing each other?'

'They've known each other for ages,' Holly had replied, 'but they've only recently got together as a couple.'

'Well, they're made for each other in my opinion.'

It was an opinion Holly shared. Harry and Amy fitted. She was thinking of the two of them as she pushed Rosie's buggy around the corner of Town Street, hoping with all her heart that the course of their love would run more smoothly than it had for her. She stopped abruptly in her tracks. Someone was knocking on the door of her house and, even from this distance, Holly was pretty sure it was Philippe. Her heart tightened in her chest. She hadn't seen or spoken to him in over a month and had been starting to doubt the strength of her feelings for him after the soulmate conversation she had with Nick. For a split second she contemplated retreating back around the corner before he saw her, but what would that achieve?

'Philippe, you look amazing,' Holly said, advancing towards him. 'Cuba obviously agreed with you. Don't tell me you've finished the new book already? Come in and I'll make you a coffee. If you can help me with the buggy, we might be able to get a few minutes to ourselves before Rosie wakes up for her tea. She's shattered, bless her, after the funeral yesterday,' Holly rambled on, feeling ridiculously nervous.

'I heard about your mother from Jo. I'm sorry for your loss,' Philippe said, reaching down to lift the buggy from the footrest, while Holly gently tilted their daughter backwards from the handles.

'Thanks. You know better than most that Mum and I didn't exactly have the perfect mother-and-daughter relationship, but some things have come to light that have gone partway to helping me understand why she was like she was. Let's pop Rosie in here,' she said, reversing into the living room, 'and we can go through to the kitchen to talk.'

'She's even more beautiful than I remember her,' Philippe said, half to himself, a hint of sadness in his voice. 'It's good to see you both,' he added, but it was lost on Holly who was already in the kitchen filling the kettle with water.

'So, when did you get back?'

'First thing this morning. I'm expecting the jet lag to kick in any moment.'

'I think I've become immune to it with all the travelling for Soleil.'

'How was your trip to Mexico?'

'Short,' Holly said. 'I came back early when I found out Mum was really sick in hospital. Thank God I did or my lasting memory of her would have been the vitriolic comment she made to me at my dad's graveside. At least I feel we had the chance to forgive each other.'

Philippe was silent. Holly thought he must be contemplating the strained relationship he shared with his own mother. Maybe some good will come of all this, she thought, if Philippe and his mum can reconcile before it's too late.

'I got the ring,' Philippe said suddenly.

Holly was taken aback.

'Right. About that.' She'd had plenty of time to consider how she could rectify her impulsive action of returning the engagement ring after suspecting Philippe of cheating on her. She had decided to tell him she had accidentally sealed the envelope omitting to put in a note suggesting that if he proposed to her properly, she would accept. It was a lie, but one she was prepared to tell for Rosie's sake. 'I—'

Philippe raised his hand to stop her speaking.

'It's okay. I've had time to think clearly while I've been holed up in Cuba, writing. You're right, Holly. It's never going to work between us.'

Holly felt as though she had been struck. She could feel the blood pumping through her veins and her peripheral vision started to go hazy. Please don't faint, she thought, gripping on to the side of the kitchen table. In all the times she had played out this scene in her head, this had never been an option. Philippe loved her. He'd told her so time and time again. This couldn't be happening.

'I'm sorry,' he continued. 'I'm just not cut out to be

a family man. I'm too selfish. I've loved these past three weeks, getting up in the morning and going straight to my computer to write. And in the evening, after I'd written my five or six thousand words, I could relax by having wine or beer with my dinner and sometimes cocktails afterwards. On a couple of occasions, I got quite drunk, and you know what? I enjoyed it. I understood your reasons for not wanting to live with a drinker and I tried to stick to your rules because I really wanted to be with you. But I can't do it. I can't spend the rest of my life scared of getting tipsy in case you throw me out.'

Philippe reached his hand across the table but Holly withdrew hers as though the touch had scalded her. Tears pricked her eyes. She bit down on her lip, resolutely refusing to cry. He used the past tense, she thought. He had definitely said, 'I really wanted to be with you.' His mind was made up. There were no more second chances.

Philippe looked spent. 'You've been strong and made the right decision for both of us, and for that I admire you. I don't need to know your reasons, but I do agree with you.'

Holly was shell-shocked. She had been about to suggest they get married. How can I have let this happen? she thought, her heart pounding.

'Wh-what about Rosie? You will want to see her, won't you? She will grow up knowing her dad?'

Philippe looked into Holly's eyes, then turned his head away to hide his agony.

'I don't know, Holly. I think we both want what's best for Rosie and I'm not sure that includes me. You did an amazing job bringing up Harry on your own and I know you can do it again, only this time you won't have to worry about money, I promise. I've never pictured myself as a Saturday dad, only there for trips to the zoo and the pizza restaurant, which is why I've made another big decision.'

Holly, still reeling from the shock, was barely breathing. How much worse can this get? she thought.

'I've been offered a deal with a big American publishing company and I've accepted it. I'm going to live in the States. I leave at the end of the week.'

'Just like that? No discussion? You're abandoning us?'

'That's not fair, Holly, and you know it. There were only so many hoops I could jump through before I started to feel like a performing animal in the circus. And besides, you made your feelings quite clear when you returned the ring.'

'Well,' Holly said, taking a deep breath, 'I guess it's better that this has happened now rather than a couple of years down the line. Divorce can be so messy. I think I want you to go now before Rosie wakes up. There's no point in her becoming attached to someone who isn't going to feature in her life. At a later date, we can discuss her maintenance allowance and whether you'll want access to see her at all before you leave for the States.'

Philippe rose slowly from the table. 'As you wish, Holly,' he said, resignation in his voice. 'Don't hate me. I'll always love you, both of you, but I don't think I could have lived with your rules.'

Holly said nothing. She followed him to the front door and closed it behind him, then she slid down it and slumped forward, her body convulsed with huge gulping sobs.

When Rosie woke for her tea thirty minutes later, Holly had to be firm with herself. What she really wanted to do was hug her child tightly against her chest, as she had done with her teddy on the many occasions her mother had upset her as a child, but she didn't want to frighten the little girl. Instead, she carried on as normal, making her tea of boiled egg and soldiers, and playing with her before bathtime. Rosie's usual bedtime was 7 p.m. but she was still weary after the change in routine the previous day. She was yawning and clearly ready for bed by 6.30 p.m. and was asleep the moment her little blond head hit the pillow.

Holly pulled the door to her daughter's room closed and headed downstairs, wondering how best to keep herself occupied as the solitary evening stretched ahead of her. Her eyes rested on the battered white briefcase she had brought back from her mother's house the previous week. *At least it will keep my mind off things,* she thought, retrieving the key from the mantle shelf and inserting it into the lock, again marvelling that there was no hint of a musty odour as she lifted the lid and set about checking what was in all the packages, carefully protected by plastic.

Amongst various life assurance policies that hadn't been paid into since her father had died and were probably barely worth the paper they were written on, Holly discovered her parents' wills. She was thankful that her dad had been so organised, it would make dealing with her mother's estate easier. She would contact the solicitor named on the documents the following day; it all seemed pretty straightforward. If Holly's dad died first, everything would pass to his wife, and the same vice versa. In the event of both of their deaths, Holly was named as the sole beneficiary. We'll see about that, Holly thought. There may not be much to share but she was determined to halve everything there was with Helen.

The phone started to ring and Holly snatched it up, hoping that it hadn't disturbed Rosie.

'Hello, Holly?'

'Helen. That's odd, I was just thinking about you. Is everything okay?'

'Not really. I've just got back from the police station.'

'What were you doing there? Did someone break into the house?'

'No. I went to report an unlawful killing.'

Holly gripped the phone receiver tightly. 'What are you talking about, Helen?'

'I found out who had been providing Mum with whisky. Well, I say I found out but, to be more accurate, she came knocking on the door. She tried to hide the plastic bag with the bottles in it when I answered the door instead of Mum, but I was too quick for her. She obviously knew our normal routine because she called when I would usually have been out at the shops.'

'Who is she?' Holly asked, swallowing hard.

'Mrs Ellery, the social worker, the one I told you I didn't like.'

'Oh my God. That's awful. She's the last person in the world I would have suspected. Did you confront her?'

'Yes. She told me that Mum contacted her begging her to bring whisky to the house but I find that hard to believe. Mum told me she never wanted to set eyes on her again after overhearing our heated exchange in the hospital.'

'Did she go to the police station with you?'

'No. She was pretty shaken up. She more or less ran down the path and drove off in her car, but now I've given the police her details I expect they'll have her in for questioning. One thing she said, I found particularly shocking. She admitted her own mother was an alcoholic and wished there had been someone like her around to put her out of her misery. How dreadful is that?'

Holly didn't know what to say. In some respects, she could empathise with Mrs Ellery. It was hard growing up with a drunk for a mother, but helping someone to take their own life? Then Holly remembered the deception she and Rosemary had practised on an unsuspecting Robert. They had been on their way to a euthanasia clinic in Switzerland when Rosemary had slipped quietly away. Maybe their mother had asked for help to commit suicide in the only way she knew how? They would never be certain of the truth, now that she was dead.

'Are you still there, Holly?'

'Yes, sorry. It just brought back some unhappy memories. I guess we'll have to leave it to the police to sort out. I wonder if it will affect the life assurance policies, not that they are worth much, if there is any suggestion that Mum took her own life? I found a couple in the white case, along with Mum and Dad's wills. I'd just finished going through it when you rang. Hold on a minute, there's something in the bottom not wrapped in plastic.'

'What is it?' Helen asked.

'It's a brown envelope,' Holly said, cradling the phone between her shoulder and her ear so she could turn it over in her hands, 'with no writing on it.'

'Is there anything inside it?'

Holly was already lifting the flap and withdrawing a neatly folded piece of paper.

'Yes there is. That's odd, it looks like a birth certificate.' Her eyes scanned the neat writing. 'I don't understand.'

'Whose birth certificate is it, Holly?'

Holly's blood had turned to ice in her veins. 'There must be some mistake. It has my dad listed as the father and our mum as the mother and it's my birthdate but it says "male" under sex of the baby. No, it can't be…'

'What?'

Suddenly things became crystal clear for Holly. Her mother had mentioned a baby called Nicholas or Richard on her deathbed, who had been taken away. Nick was from Nottingham and had told her he was adopted as a baby because his real mother couldn't cope. They shared the same birthday. Holly let out a small strangled cry.

'Holly, what is it?'

'I think Nick is my twin brother.'

CHAPTER 40

Holly strapped Rosie into her car seat and headed for the M4 going west. She had no idea how she had managed to get through the past three days.

On Wednesday morning, her first waking thought was that she needed to see Harry, then she remembered he had exams every day for the remainder of the week which was why Carol's funeral had been arranged for Monday. She had texted him, not trusting herself to speak on the phone without crying, to ask if it would be okay for her and Rosie to visit him in Bath that weekend.

He replied,

'course - u can have my room at the flat & I'll stay at Amy's. Jack's away & Hugo said it's fine xx'.

The thought of seeing her son had sustained her through the dragging hours of Wednesday and Thursday, although at least she had used the time productively to go through the boxes of books she had brought back from her mother's. In the end there hadn't been many she had wanted to keep and the remainder she re-packed for Amy to look through.

Friday had been the usual chaotic schedule of going to the television studios from Robert's while he took care of Rosie. Holly was relieved that Nick was still away on business in Hong Kong. Since discovering the birth certificate in the bottom of the white case, Holly had stressed about whether or not she should tell him. Nick had made it clear that he had no interest in finding out about his birth mother, but Holly couldn't imagine meeting up with him on a regular basis at Robert's house without revealing that they were closely related. It was unthinkable, and Robert was inadvertently making the whole situation much worse. He had been dropping unsubtle hints about Nick 'liking' her, after she'd told him about Philippe bowing out of her life. What were the chances of a twin brother she didn't even know she had, coming to live in the same village as her friend? You'd get better odds on winning the jackpot on the National Lottery, she thought, and that's saying something.

She checked her watch. Eleven o'clock. Philippe would already be airborne, heading for his new start in America. After the initial devastation she felt when he walked out of her house and her life on Tuesday afternoon, she had time to think things through. If she had been certain he was the person she wanted to spend the rest of her life with, she would have accepted his marriage proposal at Christmas. He was right not to try and win her back after she returned his ring. A relationship built on such shaky ground had very little chance of surviving in the long term.

Holly looked in her rear-view mirror. It was Rosie she

felt most guilty about. Having no father around made no difference to her at the moment. Providing she had familiar adults to feed her, hug her and play with her, she was happy. Happy is an understatement, Holly thought. Even Harry hadn't been such a contented baby.

Harry had always maintained not having a father hadn't affected him but recent events had filled Holly with doubt. His reluctance to commit to Amy in his first year at uni was almost certainly a direct consequence of me getting together with his dad so young, Holly thought, as she filtered into the flow of traffic joining the M4. Thankfully, he'd finally seen sense, although Holly did feel a little sorry for Jack. No one had really elaborated on the reason for his and Amy's split but his behaviour towards her in Barbados must have triggered it, Holly thought. She pressed a button on her steering wheel and the radio sprang to life. She selected a talk radio station to keep her mind occupied during the short drive to Bath.

A little over an hour later she was parking her car outside Chapters bookshop where she had arranged to meet Amy. They both agreed it seemed pointless taking the boxes of books to Amy's flat, which was the top floor of a four-storey house, to sort through when she had already asked Geoff if he would take any books that were surplus to requirements to sell on his second-hand shelves. It made much more sense for Amy to go through the titles in the bookshop and simply take home any she wanted.

The buzzer sounded as Holly pushed the door open.

'Holly,' Amy exclaimed, coming out from behind the counter, 'you made good time, we weren't expecting you just yet. Put the kettle on Geoff,' she called, 'Holly's here.'

Moments later, Geoff emerged from the small room at the back of his shop. 'Yes, boss,' he said, doing a mock bow in Amy's direction. 'Ah, this must be Rosie. I've heard a lot about you, young lady.'

'Hello, Geoff, how are you? Thanks for agreeing to take any books Amy and I can't find a home for.'

'No problem. We've got plenty of space and the money I take from selling them I'll put in the charity box. Will she let me hold her?'

'I didn't think you liked babies, Geoff,' Amy remarked, as Holly handed over a willing Rosie.

'I don't like them when they are crying, disturbing my customers while they are trying to select a book. And I especially don't like toddlers who are allowed to run riot by irresponsible parents, putting their sticky fingers all over my stock. But you're not in either category, are you, Rosie?' he cooed.

'Rosie claims another scalp,' laughed Amy. 'I'll help you fetch the boxes in from the car, Holly. It seems Geoff is otherwise occupied.'

'Is she allowed to have a chocolate biscuit?' Geoff asked.

'No, she's too young. I'll bring her rusks in and you can give her one of those, then you'll really cement your friendship.'

'We're doing pretty well already,' Geoff said, allowing Rosie to play with the colourful lanyard around his neck that held his reading glasses. 'I'm quite happy for you to leave her here with me and Amy if you and Harry want to go and have a pub lunch somewhere.'

'Maybe another time, Geoff. She likes to have a sleep in the afternoon and the buzzer might disturb her. I should imagine Saturday is your busiest day, isn't it?'

Geoff gestured around the empty shop. 'Normally I'd say yes but, as you can see, we're not exactly rushed off our feet. We're eagerly awaiting the release of Philippe's next book so we can have a repeat performance of his book signing. That's the best day of business I've had in years. You could have brought him with you, Holly, it might have pulled a few customers in.'

There was an awkward silence before Holly said, 'Actually, Geoff, we're not together any more.'

'Oh, I'm sorry. Amy didn't tell me,' he said, shooting Amy an accusatory glare.

Amy shook her head slightly.

'I haven't had chance to tell Harry and Amy yet. It's very recent and I didn't want to bother them during their exams. We're fine. It's all very amicable. Come on Amy, let's get those books.'

It had taken thirty minutes to wrestle Rosie from Geoff's arms, particularly as the little girl seemed reluctant to let go of her new friend, but eventually Holly was able to get away from Chapters, leaving Amy and Geoff squabbling over books like a pair of eight-year-olds. Holly was anxious to talk to Harry about the discovery she had made earlier in the week. He was waiting for her at the front door of his building, so clearly Amy had phoned or texted to say they were on their way. Holly wondered if she had also mentioned the split with Philippe.

She stepped out of the car and Harry put his arms around her and asked, 'Are you okay?'

'Amy told you then?'

'Yes. What happened?'

'What is it they say in football when they sack a manager? By mutual consent? It was kind of like that. I've been unsure about my feelings towards Philippe for a while and he's finally admitted he's not really a family man. I won't lie, I was upset at first, but honestly, now I think it's for the best.'

'Do you mean that? I must confess to feeling a bit guilty after being partly responsible for getting you two back together.'

'You shouldn't feel guilty. If we hadn't tried to make a go of things I would always have wondered what might have been.'

'What about Rosie?' Harry asked, a noticeable edge to his voice. 'You're not going to let him just walk away from his responsibilities as a father, are you?'

Holly cleared her throat. 'Well, he certainly won't be visiting every weekend if that's what you mean. As we speak, Philippe is on a flight to America. He's signed a contract with Parrot Publications, one of America's biggest publishing companies, and he's decided to go and live there. Jo seems to think the whole Cuba experience has brought out a bit of the Ernest Hemingway in him. We've spoken about him having access to see Rosie but we haven't finalised any details yet. We're both determined she should know from the start who her daddy is, and we want to keep it out of the hands of lawyers if at all possible.'

'Sensible, so long as you can agree to remain friendly,' Harry said, pushing open the door of the first-floor living room with his foot and placing Rosie's car seat next to the sofa. 'Sit down and I'll make you a cup of tea. I got some camomile and honey in for you, if you fancy?'

'That would be lovely,' Holly said, lifting Rosie out of the car seat. 'And can you put some boiling water in a jug or something to warm Rosie's bottle? Geoff was feeding her rusks at the shop so I reckon she'll have her milk and then go down for a nap.'

Harry flicked the switch on the kettle and got two mugs and a glass jug out of the cupboard. 'Speaking of fathers, have you spoken to Gareth recently?'

'Not since my few days down in Wales. He's okay, isn't he?' Holly asked, suddenly concerned that her rejection of his advances might have had an adverse effect on his mental state.

'More than okay, I'd say. He's finally started dating Megan. At long last he's noticed what was right under his nose.'

Holly felt a pang of something that she sincerely hoped wasn't remorse. Not so long ago, Gareth had sworn his undying love for her and tried to kiss her. She had rejected his advances knowing that her future with Philippe was in doubt. Why then did she feel just the tiniest bit jealous of Megan?

'You're a fine one to talk. I suppose you could say like father, like son. How are things with you and Amy?'

'Fantastic. She's everything I could possibly want from a girlfriend and more. What an idiot I was letting Jack steal her in the first place.'

'Maybe the timing wasn't right for you two when you first met. You're just lucky fate has given you another opportunity. Does Jack know you're an item?'

'Yes. We both wanted to tell him as soon as we got together, and he was really happy for us.'

'That's a relief. He's been a good friend to you and Hugo. Is Hugo in, by the way?'

'No. He'll be back later. Did Amy mention I'm going to cook dinner for us all before I go back to hers tonight?'

'What do you mean all? I thought you said Jack was away?'

'He is. All, as in you, me, Amy, Hugo and Geoff. There you go. Hot flavoured water. Where's Rosie's bottle?'

'In the front pocket of the baby bag. If you pass the bag to me I'll change her nappy while her milk is warming, then she'll be ready for her nap. Do you think you, Jack and Hugo will stay friends when you've finished uni?'

'Definitely. Hugo's talking about us maybe going back to Barbados for a holiday again this year. He said you're invited, but I guess it depends on your schedule at *On The Sofa*. His parent's divorce is underway so at least there won't be any more attempts at reconciliation. I often wonder how they managed to stay together as long as they did. They really weren't a very good match.'

Holly supressed a smile. Her son had been dating Amy for two weeks and suddenly he was a relationship expert.

Rosie's eyelids were starting to close as she finished the final few drops of formula. Holly was able to put her straight down for a sleep in her travel cot, which Harry had erected in his bedroom while his baby sister had been enjoying her lunch.

'You are lucky, Mum,' Harry said, as Holly turned the baby-monitoring device on. 'I bet there won't be a sound out of her for a couple of hours. Amy and I couldn't believe how well behaved she was for us while you were in Mexico. I hope we'll be as lucky when we start having babies.'

Holly desperately wanted to advise against starting a family too quickly. They need to get to know each other first, enjoy being together with just the two of them, and I should know, she thought, it's a mistake I've managed to duplicate in my life. Instead, she said, 'She really is an angel but I expect that will all change when she starts teething. Actually, I'm glad we've got a couple of hours with just the two of us, Harry, there's something I need to talk to you about. It's been quite a week and I don't just mean what's happened with Philippe.'

'Go on.'

'How much have you and Nick talked? Not about work, I mean about personal stuff?'

'Well, I know he's from Nottingham and he's divorced with twin boys. Oh, and he's going to be forty in June, just like you. Maybe you two should have a joint party?' Harry said, chuckling. 'Does turning forty make you officially old?'

Holly would normally join in Harry's fun but her face was serious. 'Did you know he's adopted?'

'No, I didn't,' Harry said, surprise registering in his voice. 'I expect he'll open up to me a lot more when we start going on trips together. He seems really nice. I must admit I was a bit jealous of him at first. It felt like he was being given the Philmore Hotel project after all my hard work but Robert was just making sure I wasn't taking on too much while I was working for my exams. You know I still have to pinch myself at how lucky I've been to walk into this amazing job straight from uni, and it's all down to you and your life as a secret blogger. If you hadn't been in Mauritius checking out the Plantation House Hotel when Robert and Rosemary were staying as guests, none of this would have happened. I'm so grateful, Mum.'

'That's what mums are for and anyway, although luck played a part, if you weren't any good Robert wouldn't have offered you a job.'

'True,' Harry said, not sounding in the least bit conceited. 'I think the three of us will make an excellent team with Robert holding the fort at home while Nick and I go off on site inspections. He's due back from Hong Kong on Monday, I can't wait to hear all about it.'

'Has it ever struck you that Nick and me are quite alike?' Holly asked.

Harry shrugged. 'Not especially. Mind you, now I come to think of it, you both have dark curly hair and green eyes, and you both blush when you're embarrassed. What are you getting at?'

'Do you remember in the hospital when my mother got confused and was talking about a baby called Nicholas or Richard being taken away from her?'

'And?' Harry said, a puzzled look on his face.

'When I was going through her things, I found a birth certificate in the bottom of a case full of papers. My mum and dad were the baby's parents and the date was my birthday, but the birth certificate belonged to a male child. A child called Nicholas.'

'That is a huge leap, Mum. You're not suggesting that Nick is your twin brother?'

Holly nodded. 'Think about it, Harry. It's too much of a coincidence for him not to be. The same city, the same date of birth and you just admitted we do look a bit alike. But it's the fact that my mum talked about a baby, of the same name, being taken away from her. It has to be him.'

'But why would they take him away from his mother?'

'I don't know. Maybe she couldn't cope with having twins and the authorities did it to protect Nick.'

'Can they do that?'

'I suppose if they thought he was in danger. Maybe she was neglecting him. What I can't get my head around is that nobody told me.'

'By nobody, you mean your dad?'

Holly nodded miserably. 'I thought he told me everything and now I find out he was keeping a massive secret from me.'

'Well, if you're right, and it is a huge *"if"*, he must have had his reasons, Mum. He loved you. He risked his marriage by visiting us when I was a baby. Perhaps the right moment didn't present itself. How do you tell someone that they had a twin but it was given up for adoption? He was probably worried that you would have felt racked with guilt at being the chosen one. He was trying to protect you, just as you did by not telling me that my dad abandoned us. I'm sure he would have found a way to tell you eventually, if he had lived.'

Until that moment, Holly hadn't realised the enormity of the burden her dad had carried to protect both her and her mother, and the fragile peace between them. Maybe he had hoped that eventually Carol would forgive her daughter and accept her and Harry back into the family. If he had told Holly about her twin being taken away from their mother because she had been unable to cope, it might have driven a permanent wedge between them. As it was, his death in the road accident had done that anyway.

Harry interrupted her thoughts. 'Are you going to tell Nick?'

'I don't know. He told me he wasn't interested in tracing his real mother. I don't suppose it ever occurred to him that he might have siblings, particularly not a twin. God, what a mess. The worst thing is that I feel so comfortable in his company. I had even wondered if, given time, Nick and me might have got together as a couple. What a horrific thought.'

'I didn't realise you had those kind of feelings for Nick.'

'I don't really know if I did, Harry. I was so embroiled in the whole situation with Philippe, and Nick was so kind and helpful. Not to mention that he's really good with Rosie, as you'd expect, having raised children of his own. Whatever I might have been starting to feel for him doesn't matter now, I'm just thankful I found out before things went any further.'

'Oh, Mum,' Harry said, moving over to his mother's side and pulling her into a hug, 'there is a perfect man for you out there, you just haven't found him yet.'

'I'm not so sure. As you so thoughtfully pointed out, I'm forty in a few weeks' time. Not only that, but I have a young baby, which most men of a similar age to me wouldn't necessarily see as a good thing. It's at least sixteen years of putting each other second. Not exactly appealing, is it?'

'Don't give up, Mum. You're a television personality now and you've already had loads of mail from men who think you're beautiful. One or two of them might not be nut-jobs.'

Holly, who had been on the brink of tears, pushed her son away laughing.

'There's a job for you next time you're home. You can go through all my fan mail and sort me out some eligible bachelors.'

'Really?'

'No, of course not. I'm not that desperate,' she said, adding the word 'yet' under her breath.

CHAPTER 41

Geoff screwed up his paper napkin and sat back in his seat, patting his stomach. 'Very impressive, Harry. Did your mother teach you to cook?'

'Oh, I picked up a few tips from her along the way but mostly it's the Internet. You simply type in what you fancy making and it gives you loads of alternatives and usually a step-by-step guide,' Harry said, modestly.

'It's been a nightmare sharing a house with him for the past two years,' Hugo said, a look of mock horror on his face. 'I think I must have put on a couple of stones in weight. You know he bakes cakes as well?'

'Really?'

'One cake, Hugo, get your facts straight. I made a birthday cake for my mum last year, Geoff. She normally does her own but she was away on one of her trips so I gave it a go. It wasn't half bad, as it happens.'

'It was actually better than I make and you know it,' Holly said.

'Beginner's luck. I think you're being nice about it so that I'll bake your cake this year too. Forget it, I'm not falling for it.'

'As if,' Holly smiled.

'When is your birthday, Holly?' Geoff asked.

'The nineteenth of June, and I'll save Harry the effort of trying to embarrass me by telling you how old I am. I'll be forty, Geoff,' she said, casting a 'so there' look in Harry's direction.

'Wow. You look good—'

Four pairs of eyes fixed on him in the nick of time, preventing him from saying the three words that every woman of forty plus does not want to hear.

'She does, doesn't she?' Amy piped up. 'My mum's about the same age and looks a good ten years older than you, Holly, and acts it too. She is so Edwardian when it comes to relationships. I rang to tell her about Harry and me, and all she could say was that I should be careful going from boyfriend to boyfriend or I'll get a reputation.' Amy shook her head in exasperation. 'Two boyfriends in three years of uni! It must be some kind of record.'

'It's a parent thing, Amy. We can't help worrying about our children. Do you have any children, Geoff?'

'No. It's quite a difficult thing to achieve without a woman in your life. I am thinking of kidnapping Rosie, though. What a little charmer.'

'Are all babies that well behaved?' Hugo asked, wiping a piece of ciabatta bread around his plate to soak up the last of the arrabbiata sauce.

'Nooo,' was the emphatic response from the other four adults.

Soon after dinner was finished, Holly excused herself claiming tiredness after a full-on week. Harry offered to drop Geoff home on their way back to Amy's but he declined.

'I could do with a walk in the fresh air to sober up a bit,' he admitted.

'Crikey, Geoff, you're a bit of a lightweight. You've only had two glasses of wine,' Hugo exclaimed. 'How can you possibly be drunk?'

'Not drunk, Hugo, just a little light-headed. Some of us don't have to rely on alcohol to have a good time,' he said, pointedly.

'Oh, Geoff, you have clearly forgotten your uni days. Alcohol or drugs are the only things that get most students through, not that I condone the latter. It would be a very dull time if we were just here studying,' Hugo said, taking a swig from his bottle of Peroni.

'We're not all like that,' Harry said, walking Geoff down to the front door. 'And don't be fooled by Hugo's chat, he doesn't really drink to excess either, despite all the rubbish he has to contend with courtesy of his parents. I hope you enjoyed the evening?'

'I did. The food was truly delicious and the company pretty good too. It made such a lovely change from sitting on my own in front of the television or reading a book. Your mother's a wonderful woman. Beautiful, funny, independent and, most importantly, she shares my passion for books. How come I've never been able to attract someone like her? Goodnight, Harry.'

'Night, Geoff,' Harry said, closing the door behind him before racing up the stairs two at a time. He burst into the lounge. 'You'll never guess what?'

Amy and Hugo stared blankly at him.

'I think Geoff's got a crush on my mum.'

'Oh, that is so sweet,' Amy said, 'but she really is way out of his league.'

'Do you think so?'

'Er, yes. Geoff is lovely but dull. I love books and even I find him constantly talking about them boring.'

'Yes, but you're younger, Amy. When you get to Mum's age perhaps that would be riveting conversation, and you said yourself you couldn't believe how well he got on with Rosie.'

'Please tell me you're not going to try and set them up together?'

'Gotta agree with Amy on this one,' Hugo said. 'I don't think we should interfere with our parents' affairs of the heart. Anyway, she's with that author chappie, isn't she?'

'Not any more,' Harry sighed. 'I think he's having a bit of a mid-life crisis. He's decided he's not ready to settle down and has sodded off to America. Good riddance, I say.'

'Well, I think it's a shame. They made such a stunning couple. He really was very handsome,' Amy said, a dreamy expression on her face. Hugo and Harry were staring at her. 'What?'

'You forget woman, you are spoken for,' Harry said, doing his best caveman impression and advancing across the room towards her.

Amy responded by running behind Hugo and saying, 'Save me, Hugo.'

'Oh God. I'm off to bed if you two are going to play lovey-dovey games.'

'Hey, wasn't the deal that you would do the washing-up in return for dinner and booze?'

Hugo wafted his hand, 'It'll still be there in the

morning, I'll do it then. Night.'

Amy started pushing her sleeves up and Harry grabbed a tea towel.

'You wash and I'll dry. We'll decide what your punishment for fancying Philippe is when we get back to yours,' Harry said, reaching his arms around Amy's waist and nibbling her neck.

CHAPTER 42

Helen took the final sip of her tea and placed the mug back on the slatted wooden table. I'm going to miss this garden, she thought. What a shame I didn't have time to finish all the things I wanted to do. All the spring bulbs were coming to the end of their flowering period but she wouldn't be planting out any summer bedding to replace them. Her bags were packed in the hallway. All that remained now was to hand over the keys to the man from the council housing department when he turned up.

The council had been surprisingly tolerant, saying that Helen could carry on living at the house until the end of June, but Helen knew how many families were cooped up in bed-and-breakfast accommodation so had offered to vacate the house earlier. There was nothing keeping her in Clifton. The previous week, she had applied for several jobs in care homes and was waiting to hear back about interviews. The money was pretty dreadful but all the posts she had applied for were live-in so at least she would have a roof over her head.

In the meantime, she had taken Holly up on her kind offer to stay with her in Reading for a week or so until her next trip to a far-flung place. I wonder where she's going this time, Helen mused. She herself had never set foot outside of the UK, in fact, she had only ever left England once when she went on her honeymoon to Loch Lomond, in Scotland. The private hotel was very small, only eight rooms, and it had reminded her of the comedy television show *Fawlty Towers*. The owner, Roger Pink, wasn't quite as crazy as Basil Fawlty but there was a foreign waiter who spoke virtually no English, and Mrs Pink was a bit stuck-up and unfriendly. Although they were on their honeymoon she had treated them as though they were on a dirty weekend. With the benefit of hindsight, considering Graeme was already married, we were, thought Helen.

Despite Mrs Pink's attitude towards them, Helen had a wonderful time. She had enjoyed walking hand in hand with the man she thought was her partner for life along the side of the loch, the sun sparkling off the ripples on the surface as they occasionally stopped to kiss under the boughs of large trees. They hadn't seen a drop of rain for the week they were there until the morning they left. The heavens had opened and they got drenched in the short walk from the hotel porch to the taxi that was waiting to drive them back to Glasgow station. The smell of damp wool always conjured up the memory of that train journey back to Nottingham.

It was possibly the happiest week of my life, Helen thought, and then allowed herself a 'so far' on the end. Discovering she had a half-sister and, potentially, a half-brother, had given her an incredible feeling of belonging for the first time in her life. She wasn't as totally convinced as Holly was that Nick was her twin brother. Having delved into the world of tracing family trees, Helen knew that things weren't always as straightforward as they appeared. She had every intention of checking Holly's discovery out thoroughly once she had got herself settled in a new position.

There was a knock at the front door. This is it, Helen thought, another new beginning. She took a final lingering look at the garden she had begun to love, picked up her mug and rinsed it quickly under the kitchen tap. A wipe with a piece of kitchen towel and it was ready to be squeezed into the corner of her suitcase before she zipped it closed.

CHAPTER 43

Holly was hoping she had done the right thing as her taxi pulled away from the kerb at 6.30 on Friday morning to take her from Reading to the television studios. Inside her house she had left both her daughter and her sister fast asleep, although it wouldn't be long before Helen would start to hear sounds of activity from Rosie's cot via the baby monitor on her bedside table.

It had been a difficult decision to make on a number of levels. There was a small part of her that was nervous about leaving her precious baby daughter with someone she had met so recently, even though Helen was her own flesh and blood and she felt sure that she would never do anything to hurt her child. The two of them had been getting on famously since Helen's arrival in Reading four days prior and with her previous employment in the special needs baby unit she was perfectly able to care for eight-month-old Rosie.

Then there was Robert. Holly hadn't wanted to disappoint him. He had become used to having his young charge to look after on Friday mornings while Holly was at the television studios. In many respects it was the highlight of his week. When Holly had rung to say she wouldn't be taking Rosie across to his house that week, the disappointment in his voice was acute. Holly had to think on her feet. Her main reason for not going to Woldingham was to avoid Nick who was now back from Hong Kong. If she invited Robert over to visit Rosie at her house, he would be happy because he would get cuddles with his little princess and Holly would also be more at ease. It did occur to Holly that Helen might view it as a lack of trust but it was a risk worth taking.

Robert wasn't due to arrive until 9 a.m. but if Holly knew him as well as she thought she did, she reckoned he would be parked outside by 8 a.m. at the latest with some excuse about there being less traffic than he had expected.

Helen and Robert hadn't met in person, although they had exchanged a few words on the phone. It would be an interesting first encounter, Holly thought, especially as Robert had made no attempt to hide the reservations he felt about Holly accepting her half-sister into the bosom of her family so readily.

She settled back into the comfortable leather seats of the taxi for the journey to London, wondering what excuse she would give for not wanting to stay at Robert's once her sister had moved on. Nick was not stupid. It wouldn't take him long to realise she was avoiding him and when he questioned her about it, what was she going to say?

CHAPTER 44

Holly had slept for most of the journey, as she often did on long-haul flights, waking only to eat and use the bathroom. She felt surprisingly fresh as she gathered together her belongings to disembark the Cathay Pacific plane at Chek Lap Kok airport. She had never travelled to the Far East before so was eager for her first experience of the Orient.

Holly had originally been scheduled to visit Egypt but, after a spate of terrorist attacks, Soleil had changed her booking at the last minute. When she had received their email advising her of the revised destination she had felt excitement and dread in equal measure. Hong Kong was a place she had always wanted to visit after devouring James Clavell's *Tai-Pan* and *Noble House*. The fly in the ointment was that having very recently returned from there himself, it would seem really odd for her not to speak to Nick about his impressions of the former colony and pick his brains on places to visit. Odd or not, she had maintained her distance. Holly knew she would eventually have to broach the subject of being siblings with Nick but, feeling fragile after her mother's death and the split with Philippe, she couldn't trust herself not to break down in tears.

Having Helen at her house in Reading was a reasonable excuse not to visit Woldingham, and thus not bump into Nick, but Robert had missed having Rosie to stay and so had hatched a plan. While Holly was at *On The Sofa* and Robert was visiting Reading for the second Friday running, he suggested to Helen that she might like to stay at Valley View for the six days Holly was away in Hong Kong, rather than being on her own in Reading.

'You and Rosie can come back to my house tonight, when Holly leaves for the airport, and she can get a taxi to mine, rather than Reading, when she gets back next Thursday. It's a much easier journey from Woldingham to the television studios than it is from here and I expect she'll be really tired after all that travelling. Maybe you could suggest it to her? She's always putting others before herself so if she thinks it's something you would like to do, she's more likely to say yes.'

Robert had used his considerable charm on Helen, which hadn't really been necessary. She had been longing to visit Valley View since Holly had shown her some photographs of Robert's beautiful Surrey home.

Holly hadn't needed much persuading either. She liked the idea of two people being around to care for Rosie and she could use the excuse that she hadn't seen her little house for a week to leave straight after lunch on Friday, minimising any potential contact with Nick.

'Your passport please, and look into the camera.'

Holly had reached the front of the queue at passport control very quickly. You have to admire the efficiency of the Chinese, she thought, handing her passport over.

'The purpose of your visit?'

This was always a tricky one for Holly. Technically she was working but she had been instructed by Soleil to say pleasure. Holly hated lying and was always fearful of the tell-tale blush giving the game away. She smiled inwardly. At least I would never attempt to be a drug smuggler, she thought. That would be the easiest arrest in history.

'Business or pleasure,' the border control officer prompted.

'Oh, um, pleasure,' she faltered.

The officer looked at her for a moment longer than was comfortable and she could feel the heat of a blush starting.

'Enjoy your stay,' he said, waving her through.

Holly breathed a sigh of relief as she tucked her passport back into her crossbody bag and re-joined the throng of arrivals making their way towards baggage reclaim. She could imagine Nick's reaction to the airport when he had arrived three weeks ago. The structure was very impressive, constructed mostly in glass with a huge vaulted ceiling, allowing the natural light into the building but with vast air-conditioning units keeping the heat out.

In the guidebook Holly had been reading at Heathrow Airport it had advised that May through to August weren't the best months to travel to Hong Kong. It was hot, with very high humidity and an ever-present risk of typhoons. She couldn't imagine many British holidaymakers venturing so far with such unpredictable weather at the end of their journey, but Soleil was international so there would be no shortage of tourists from other parts of the Far East.

Many people journeyed to Hong Kong for business, shopping or as a stopover en route to destinations such as Australia and New Zealand, but the hotel Holly was visiting had been acquired by Soleil with the intention of enticing holidaymakers to stay for a week or two and discover that Hong Kong had so much more to offer than towering skyscrapers and neon lights. It was situated on the south coast of Hong Kong Island not far from Stanley with its bustling market, something else she had learned about from the guidebook. I really didn't need to pick up any tips from Nick, she thought, wheeling her suitcase towards the row of drivers with name boards who were lining the exit route.

Holly spotted her surname.

'Mrs Wilson?' the driver said as she approached.

'Yes,' Holly replied.

'Let me take your bag. Follow me. Is this your first time in Hong Kong?'

Holly experienced déjà vu of all the times she had been met by dozens of welcoming drivers over the months she had been working for Soleil, who always greeted her with the same question.

'Yes it is. How far is it to the hotel?'

'It's a long way, but I can tell you plenty about Hong Kong if you have questions. I've lived here all my life, I'm not from China.'

Holly detected a note of pride in the man's voice as she followed him towards the exit doors. He is going to be a mine of useful information, she thought as the sliding doors opened and she stepped out into the damp heat of Saturday afternoon.

By the time she was checking in at her hotel, almost two hours later, Holly had had a potted history of Hong Kong. Some of the stories she already knew from the fiction she had read, but the recent history was equally as interesting.

The airport she had landed at was a relatively new addition, opening in 1996. As the size of planes had increased, the urgency to replace Kai Tak on the mainland, which had a very short runway, grew. The answer had been to move it out of the built-up areas and build a new road network to transport visitors into the commercial districts. According to Chi, her driver, the small island of Chek Lap Kok, situated off the coast of the largest of the Hong Kong island group, Lantau, had been completely flattened to accommodate the airport buildings and runways. Chi's family were from Lantau and although they were grateful for the jobs the new airport had created in their area, they were sad at the destruction it had also brought.

'When I was a boy, the only way to the island from Hong Kong was by boat, one hour or an hour and a half. There were no tall buildings here. My father was a fisherman and we had a very simple life. Now it's all changed,' he said.

It certainly had, Holly thought. The airport island was linked to Lantau by a bridge and another much longer bridge linked it to the mainland. There seemed to be fast-moving American-style highways going in all directions.

'What should I visit while I'm here?' Holly had ventured at one point.

'The Peak, to give you fantastic views, Stanley market, which is close to you at Repulse Bay, and maybe Happy

Valley racecourse.'

Holly had been disappointed with his response. He had named the usual suspects when it came to sightseeing in Hong Kong and she had hoped to tap into his local knowledge. Oh well, she thought, climbing into the lift to take her to the fourteenth floor of her hotel, I'll have to rely on the information dished out at the welcome meeting tomorrow morning. She tipped the porter thirty Hong Kong dollars, locked the door behind him and slipped her feet out of her shoes. She lay down on the gold and green counterpane of her huge queen-size bed and wiggled her toes. Bliss, she thought, closing her eyes for a few moments.

CHAPTER 45

Helen awoke later than usual on Saturday morning, making her late down for breakfast. Robert had insisted that he should have the baby monitor overnight, pointing out that if Rosie needed some milk or a nappy change in the early hours, Helen wouldn't know where anything was. Consequently, Robert and Rosie had already been up for a couple of hours before Helen surfaced.

'Sorry,' she said apologetically, making her way down the sweeping staircase, 'I should have set my alarm.'

'What for?' Robert asked. 'Nothing's spoiling. We have the whole day to do exactly as we choose, although Nick is popping in this morning to bring me up to speed on the Hong Kong project. The coffee is still fairly fresh or I can make a new pot. What do you fancy for breakfast? Toast? Cereal?'

Helen wasn't listening. She had walked over to the full-length windows and was standing transfixed, gazing down the garden.

'Oh my God. I think I've died and gone to heaven.'

Robert winced, but Helen was totally unaware of what

she had said.

'That is the most beautiful garden I've ever seen,' she gushed. 'Can I go outside for a closer look?'

'Of course,' Robert said, retrieving the key from the drawer in the coffee table. 'It's a shame it's not quite as warm as it looks or you could have had your breakfast out there.' He unlocked the door and stood aside to let Helen pass, then followed her out with Rosie on his hip.

'I've always dreamed of having a garden like this,' she said, crossing the patio and dropping the four steps on to the lawn, which was looking lush despite the ravages of winter. 'It's immaculate. Do you tend it yourself, Robert?'

'I'm afraid I can't lay claim to it. I have a gardener who comes once a fortnight in winter and once a week in the summer, although now that Rosemary's not here that may not be enough,' Robert said.

'Oh gosh, Robert, how thoughtless of me, I hope I didn't upset you,' Helen said.

'It's fine. It's almost a year since my wife died and I still think about her every single day. People say time is a great healer but I'm not sure I want to be healed. I overheard Holly and Nick talking about soulmates the other day and that's what Rosemary was to me. She was my life, my everything. I existed to make her happy and when she went, I struggled with my purpose in life until this little lady showed up,' he said, affectionately pulling Rosie's nose between his finger and his thumb, pretending that his thumb was her nose.

Helen watched Robert put the 'nose' back on Rosie's face, much to the little girl's delight.

'I know what you mean. If it hadn't been for the support of friends, I might have looked for solace at the bottom of a wine bottle. It would seem I really am my mother's daughter. It wasn't easy overcoming the shock and the grief but I think going in search of my mother gave me back my purpose.'

'When did you lose your husband, Helen?'

'Six years ago.'

'So young. At least I'm in my sixties; you had half your life ahead of you. Did you ever think about looking for someone else?'

'It's not that easy, Robert. Take a look at me. I'm clearly the ugly duckling in the family. The other two are the image of their father and he was a very handsome man.'

Robert was puzzled. 'I thought Holly was an only child, well, until she discovered you of course?'

Brushing over her slip of the tongue, Helen said, 'You know, you're right, it is a bit nippy out here. Let's get Rosie indoors, we don't want Holly coming back to a poorly baby.'

Ten minutes after Helen had strapped Rosie into her buggy to take her for a walk into the village to buy some fresh bread for lunch, Robert heard the crunch of tyres on the gravel driveway. He went through to the kitchen to put the kettle on and moments later Nick's head appeared around the edge of the door.

'Tea?' Robert asked.

'You know me too well. Was that Rosie I saw out in her buggy? Who was she with?'

'That's Helen, Holly's sister. Very nice woman, as it happens.'

Nick smiled. 'Do I remember you suggesting to Holly

that she might be an axe murderer?'

'That's not what I said and you know it. I was merely concerned for Holly putting too much trust in someone she barely knows. It doesn't hurt to be cautious.'

'I was teasing, Robert. I'm all for protecting Holly. She's had a pretty torrid time of it lately.'

'Indeed she has. And now Philippe walking out on her just when she needs someone to lean on. It's a good job she's got Harry, and me of course to a lesser extent.'

'When did all this happen?' Nick asked.

'While you were away in Hong Kong.'

'Is that why she's been avoiding me since I got back?'

'Oh, I don't think she's been avoiding you. She's a very busy woman and she's had Helen staying with her.'

'She definitely has. I tried to call her yesterday to make some suggestions of places she might like to visit in Hong Kong but it went straight to voicemail.'

'Did you leave a message for her to ring you back?'

'No. But I tried her three or four times.' Nick was crossing his fingers. He had actually tried to call Holly a dozen or more times. The excuse about sharing ideas for places to see in Hong Kong was to get her to speak to him. There was something important he wanted to tell her.

'Maybe her phone was off. She probably has to turn it off at the studios and may have forgotten to put it back on. Anyway, what were you doing sightseeing on company time?' Robert teased.

'A man has to eat, you know. How funny that Holly's destination was changed from Egypt to Hong Kong but such a shame that we weren't there at the same time.'

Robert was observing Nick closely. He had long

suspected that Nick had a soft spot for Holly but had kept his distance because of Philippe. Now that Philippe was out of the picture maybe the two of them would get together. He recalled the conversation he had with Holly on the day of her *On The Sofa* debut as they walked through Battersea Park. 'Resist the urge to meddle,' was what she had said to him about Harry and Amy. He had shown remarkable restraint and the two of them had got together just fine. But Holly was a different kettle of fish. Would it really hurt that much if he gave nature a bit of a helping hand? Robert handed Nick his cup of tea.

'Let's go through to the office and have a look at the project,' Robert said, the germ of an idea starting in his brain. 'It's quite a complex one. I hope you haven't missed anything.'

CHAPTER 46

Holly was shattered. Hong Kong seemed such a small place when you looked at it on a map but there was certainly no shortage of things to do, and trying to pack as much as possible into six days was proving exhausting. Not for the first time Holly had to question how much longer she would be able to keep up her hectic Liberty Sands schedule now that she had the time restraints of appearing on television every Friday morning. She had also realised it was unfair to travel with Rosie on the more distant trips and she missed her baby dreadfully. It was some comfort knowing she was in capable, loving hands but that did nothing to diminish the overwhelming desire for a cuddle with her daughter.

She shuffled forward in the queue waiting to board the Star Ferry to travel back across the harbour to Hong Kong Island. It was like a bus service ploughing across the congested waterway every few minutes. The advice at the welcome meeting on her first morning had been to pay the extra money to travel on the upper deck of the ferry as most tourists did. In the interests of research Holly had ignored the advice and travelled on the lower deck to have an authentic experience. She regretted it. The crossing had been punctuated by people clearing their throats and spitting into spittoons. Needless to say the ticket she was clutching in her hand for the return journey was an upgrade for the top deck.

People began swarming up the ramp on the other side of the metal railing and no sooner had all the passengers disembarked than a bell sounded and the queue on Holly's side of the railing moved forward at pace. Within minutes the ferry cast off once more heading into the incongruous mix of luxury yachts and traditional junks and sampans that dotted the harbour.

The previous day, Holly had been on a day trip on a junk, organised by the hotel, visiting some of the other islands and then dropping anchor at Deep Water Bay for lunch. Post lunch, some of the guests stretched out on the deck in the warm sun while others opted to swim. Holly slipped into the cool navy water for respite from the heavy heat but didn't stay in long. The water was very salty and felt almost stinging against her skin. It was an enjoyable day and gave her the opportunity to mingle with other hotel guests who were interested in more than merely shopping for replicas of big brand names, but Holly didn't rate it very highly on value for money.

Daylight was fading fast as the ferry approached the shore and as it did the neon lights on Hong Kong Island sprang into life, illuminating the crush of buildings reaching up towards the inky sky against the backdrop of Victoria Peak. Holly glanced at her watch. The taxi ride back to her hotel from the ferry terminal would take around thirty minutes. She definitely needed a refreshing shower after indulging in a spot of retail therapy on

Granville Road but she wouldn't be able to linger or she would risk missing dinner in the main restaurant of the hotel, which didn't stay open as late as she would have expected. She had mentioned that in her first blog of the trip after being too late to get served on her first evening. The nap she had taken had stretched to three hours and she had to resort to room service. The food she couldn't fault, nor the impeccably polite service, but restaurant opening times needed to be addressed, in Holly's opinion.

Fortunately, there were plenty of cabs on the stand and it was a relief to climb into the air-conditioned interior and explore the contents of her colourful bags on the journey back to her hotel. Holly's shopping expedition had consisted of buying cute outfits for Rosie, very reasonably priced designer T-shirts for Harry and some pieces of fortune-bringing jade for Robert, Helen and Amy. She had also treated herself. Holly didn't usually get excited about handbags but she had spotted a Prada bag in a beautiful shade of periwinkle blue in a half-price sale. It may well have been reduced because it was from the previous season but that didn't bother Holly. She liked it and she deserved a treat. She could already imagine Maddie and Tamsin's faces when she turned up at the television studios with it on her shoulder on Friday.

Holly was still smiling as she walked into the hotel lobby after paying the driver.

'Holly.'

She stopped mid-stride. She could barely believe her eyes.

'I'd begun to think maybe you were staying out for dinner.'

'What are you doing here?' Holly asked as Nick slid

off his barstool, from where he had a perfect view of the entrance to the hotel, and approached her.

'It's a long story. Why don't I tell you about it over dinner? Unless you've got other plans?'

Holly felt like a rabbit in the headlights. She had managed to avoid speaking to Nick for almost a month and now he had followed her halfway around the world.

'No plans. In fact, I was worried I might be a bit late for dinner in the hotel restaurant.'

'Oh we can do better than that,' Nick smiled. 'I've got a real Hong Kong experience for you if you're interested?'

'Well…'

'It will be great on your blog,' Nick urged. 'You don't need to dress up or anything, just bring something to put around your shoulders in case it gets cooler later on.'

Holly was intrigued. How could she refuse when Nick had clearly been waiting in the hotel reception area for some time? It would be churlish.

'Okay, let me drop these off in my room and freshen up a bit. You finish your drink and I'll be down in twenty minutes.'

True to her word, Holly was back in the reception of the hotel twenty minutes later having had a lightning quick shower, changed into a fresh pair of jeans and a flowery strappy top, and applied the tiniest hint of blusher, mascara and lip gloss. She had removed the elastic band that had held her hair in a ponytail all day, keeping it off her neck, and replaced it with the sparkly Butler and Wilson hairclip she was so fond of.

'Wow, you look amazing,' Nick said, leaning in to kiss

Holly on the cheek.

She recoiled as though bitten by a snake. This is really not a good idea, Holly thought, following Nick out to the waiting taxi. I'm going to have to tell him what I've found out.

'Shun Kee, in the Causeway Bay Typhoon Shelter, please,' Nick instructed the driver.

'Is there a typhoon on the way?' Holly asked, mildly panicking.

Nick smiled. 'No. We're not going there to shelter we're going there to eat. I promise you an experience like you've never had before. You do like seafood, don't you?'

'Love it,' Holly confirmed.

'Good. So, how do you like Hong Kong so far? Is it what you expected?'

'I didn't know what to expect really. It was all so last minute. Apologies for not returning your calls, by the way, I've been up to my neck with everything and I've had Helen staying.' Holly was grateful the relative darkness in the back of the taxi was concealing her blush.

'No worries. I just thought you might like some insider information on things to do while you're here. You know, a little bit of the real Hong Kong to add flavour to your blog. Sorry. That came out a bit wrong. I didn't mean your blog is usually lacking flavour,' Nick added, somewhat flustered.

'Have you been reading my blog again?' Holly teased.

'Maybe. It's quite exciting for a boring architect to know a famous writer and television personality.'

'Hardly famous, Nick, and you're not boring at all. You and Harry are going to have a great time travelling the world for Robert. Speaking of which, why are you back here? Has something gone wrong with the project?'

'Not really. I had a meeting with Robert on Saturday morning and we went through all the data he had asked me to collect. Apparently, there were some more measurements he needed and he didn't trust anyone out here to do it properly. I suppose it's his reputation at stake if anything goes wrong further down the line due to miscalculations. Anyway, I'm not complaining. I really like it here. It's so cosmopolitan. It's as if the world has been condensed into a few square miles.'

'Where is the hotel you're refurbishing?'

'Kowloon side. It's a fabulous location right on the waterfront, not far from the Peninsula Hotel. To be honest, I don't really know why they're bothering with the alterations. The rooms are really well appointed, particularly the one they've put me in this time. I say room, it's a corner suite on the top floor with huge windows so I've got an amazing view. I guess the public areas are a bit tired-looking but it's not a huge job, just a bit of cosmetic surgery. I was surprised when Robert rang me on Sunday evening and asked if I'd be able to fly back out here last night. It's his business so it's his call. I didn't mind at all, it's given me the chance to come and track you down. There's something I need to tell you over dinner.'

Holly's heart plummeted. She was sat in the back of a taxi on her way to dinner with an extraordinarily good-looking man who was clearly interested in getting to know her better and, as bad luck would have it, just happened to be her brother. She shifted uncomfortably in her seat, edging slightly further away from Nick.

'So it was Robert who told you where I was staying.

You nearly gave me a heart attack when I heard someone call out my name in the hotel reception. You must have come straight from the airport.'

'Not quite. I dropped my bags off and had a shower and change of clothes but I didn't want to risk you having already gone out for dinner. I rang the hotel and they said they hadn't seen you since this morning so I took a punt, booked the restaurant and headed on over.'

'It had better be good after all this build up.'

'It's pretty special. I think you'll like it.'

The taxi had been crawling through the traffic for the past few minutes and the driver kept muttering under his breath.

'We're nearly there,' Nick said, barely able to conceal his excitement. 'Are you okay to get out and walk?'

'Yes. I hate sitting in traffic.'

Nick asked the driver to pull over, paid him ninety Hong Kong dollars and the two of them got out leaving the driver to battle the traffic on his own. Nick grabbed her hand and, turning his back on the skyscrapers and neon lights, headed towards the waterfront.

'Where are you taking me?' Holly asked, almost breaking into a jog to keep up with his fast pace.

'You'll see.'

CHAPTER 47

Jo read through the letter on the desk in front of her again, carefully. She needed to make sure that she wasn't burning any bridges. Satisfied with the wording, she picked up the pen she had been given to celebrate her fifteen years of service with Ripped Publishing and signed at the foot of the letter with a flourish.

The meeting with Philippe a week ago had unsettled her. She loved her job at Ripped and had worked hard to achieve her many promotions but there was nowhere else to move up to. The thought of another fifteen or twenty years of doing exactly the same job in exactly the same surroundings, luxurious as they were, suddenly seemed unthinkable.

Jo had turned forty in February and had no one to celebrate the occasion with. Her PA, Alice, had done her best, organising flowers, champagne and cake in the office, but at six o' clock the staff had all gone home, leaving Jo to a solitary evening in her penthouse apartment overlooking the River Thames. As she sat flicking through the channels on the television, eventually stopping at the shopping channel for a bit of friendly company, Jo had toyed with the idea of ringing Geoff. She turned his business card over and over in her hand before tucking it back in the pocket of her handbag. She liked Geoff, but he didn't set her world on fire. She needed someone with more get up and go, someone like Philippe. Who am I kidding? she had thought, I don't mean someone like Philippe, I mean the man himself. Jo had struggled to get past her infatuation with Philippe. Theirs was a fiery relationship, always trying to get the better of one another, but Jo found that stimulating and exciting. The thought of settling for second best merely because she didn't want to end up a sad and lonely old woman was something Jo couldn't contemplate.

Things had happened rather more quickly than she had anticipated after putting in a call to Parrot, the American publishing company that Philippe had signed his deal with. They were immediately interested in her as the editor who had discovered 'Veronica Phillips' and had been at the helm of managing the publicity campaign. Within twenty-four hours of receiving Jo's full CV, listing all the successful acquisitions she had made throughout her long and successful career with Ripped, they had made her an offer. Remembering her derision of Philippe accepting the first offer on the table, she had rejected it. Fifty thousand dollars more per annum and an apartment overlooking Central Park and Jo was ready to sign on the dotted line and leave the security of the small publishing company she had helped grow into being a significant player within the book world.

She pressed the intercom button.

'Alice, would you step in here for a moment please,' she said.

Efficient as always, Alice was in her office within thirty seconds.

'How is the Holly Wilson/Liberty Sands contract coming along?' she asked.

'Pretty much done and dusted. Holly had the television company lawyer check it over for her to make sure there was no clash of interest. There were a few minor points but nothing our legal department weren't happy to amend. I suppose they view it as good publicity for *On The Sofa*. She's signed it so it's just waiting for your signature now. It's on the top of the pile of papers for today. Shall I bring them through?'

'Yes, please. And can you pop this letter in the internal mail.'

Alice took the letter from Jo, looked down at the name on the envelope and then back up at her boss, a question in her eyes.

'Yes, Alice. I'm resigning. I wanted you to be the first to know.'

CHAPTER 48

The gentle lapping of waves against the side of the boat created a rocking motion like that of a baby's cradle and was having a similarly soothing effect on Holly as she relaxed on the soft seating, sipping a pale tea with large pieces of leaf floating in it. The Shun Kee restaurant was the twenty-first-century version of dining in the typhoon harbour at Causeway Bay.

They had been welcomed aboard the small boat by their waitress who introduced herself as Ling. The boats could each accommodate up to twelve people but Nick had paid to have it to themselves.

'What do you think?' he asked.

'It's not what I was expecting at all. When you said don't dress up, I thought maybe we were going to a noodle bar or a street market. This is fabulous. I love it.'

Ling returned with their menus and once they had placed their order, Nick filled Holly in on the background to the restaurant, which he had heard from his host when they had visited on his recent trip.

'This whole bay used to be filled with boat people. Entire families would live on a sampan of a similar size to this, and when I say entire families I mean several generations. To supplement their income, some of the families would welcome guests on to their boats and for an agreed price would cook dinner for them over a gas burner at one end of their cramped living space. Apparently it was all a bit hit and miss, with the quality of the food largely dependent on how much you tipped the taxi sampan taking you out to the cooking boats. Although tourists loved the genuine slice of local life, the authorities were growing increasingly concerned over the lack of regulation, particularly as the boats were made of wood so there was a massive potential for fire. There was also a significant health risk from the lack of sanitation and resulting polluted water. Imagine the smell in this heat.'

Holly wrinkled her nose. As Nick talked, her eyes were distracted by the bright ribbons of colour striping the water, created by the reflection of neon lights from the skyscrapers that towered high above them.

'By the nineties, the sampans and their families had been rehoused in accommodation on dry land, with running water and a sewage system, and the harbour had been cleaned up, but a piece of Hong Kong history had almost been lost for ever.'

'That would have been such a shame,' Holly said. 'Not all progress is good progress.'

'That's exactly how a former resident viewed it. He had worked as a cook on his family's boat and, such was the quality of his food, had been wooed into taking a job as a chef in one of the best restaurants in Hong Kong. He never forgot his roots and eventually, after years of red tape, won permission to open this new floating restaurant with its flotilla of small boats. What a brilliant idea.'

'Absolutely. I'm glad they've managed to revive the tradition, even if it is in a cleaned-up version,' Holly said. 'It's really quite magical.'

'I'm so pleased you like it. I hoped you would. It beats dining in the hotel, doesn't it?'

'Well I haven't tasted the food yet, but if the aromas are anything to go by it should be pretty amazing.' Holly inhaled deeply, the smell of ginger, garlic and lemongrass invading her nostrils. Her stomach grumbled. 'Oops, sorry. I hadn't realised how hungry I am and the smell is wonderful.'

Ling was approaching carrying a small plate with two bite-sized spring rolls and a couple of giant prawns as an appetiser.

'Your starter will be a few minutes,' she said, bowing slightly.

'We were just saying what a lovely idea this is. Have you worked here long?' Holly asked, reaching for a spring roll and popping it into her mouth.

'I only work here on Tuesday nights when my brother has the night off. Most of the time I work at Temple Street market.'

'Oh, I think I read about it in my guidebook,' Holly said. 'It's on Kowloon side isn't it? Do you work in a restaurant there?'

'Yes, it is in Kowloon side, but no, I don't work in a restaurant. I'm a fortune-teller.'

'How fascinating,' Holly said. 'Do you have a crystal ball?'

'No,' the waitress said smiling. 'I do my readings from the palm and from the sense of touch. May I?' she asked, reaching for Holly's hand.

'Well, I'm not sure…'

'Go on, Holly,' Nick urged, 'it will be fun.'

Holly extended her hand to the waitress, somewhat reluctantly. She wasn't sure she believed in the ability to predict the future and, even if she did, she wasn't sure she wanted to know.

Ling held Holly's hand between her own for a moment, both eyes closed as though she was concentrating, then she looked into Holly's flattened palm.

'I see words,' she said, 'lots of words, both written and spoken. And I feel great sadness. You have said goodbye to someone very recently.'

Holly was taken aback. It could simply have been a lucky guess but Ling couldn't have been more accurate. It was what she said next that rocked Holly to her core.

'I see babies. Two babies. A boy and a girl. They are twins,' she said, adjusting her gaze to look directly at Nick.

Holly gasped.

A buzzer sounded.

'I have to fetch your food. Here is my card,' she said, producing a small red business card from a pocket in her trousers. 'Come and find me tomorrow night in Temple Street and I will give you a proper reading. I give you a very good price,' she added, hurrying away to collect their freshly cooked starters.

'We should go, Holly. She certainly seems to know her stuff. She was spot on with the words and losing your mum. Beats me how she knew about my twins from looking into your palm, even if she was a little bit out on their gender.'

Holly knew the perfect opportunity had presented

itself. She was going to have to tell Nick what she had discovered in the battered white case sooner or later and it was best that he knew before he started getting any romantic notions about the two of them.

'Nick,' she started, 'there's something I have to tell you.'

'Me too. I've known for a couple of weeks but, with you avoiding me, I haven't had a chance to say anything.'

Ling was approaching with their starter.

'I hope you will enjoy it,' she said, again bowing slightly as she left.

'I think I should go first,' Holly said, worried that Nick was going to confess his attraction towards her. She needed to tell him about their family connection otherwise things would be forever awkward for the pair of them and she didn't want it to have an adverse effect on their future relationship or his ability to work comfortably alongside Harry.

'Oh, taste this, it's divine,' he said, holding his chopsticks out for Holly.

She leaned in and accepted the proffered food. The flakes of fish dissolved in her mouth with an explosion of taste.

While she still had her mouth full of food, Nick seized the opportunity. 'I listened to what you said and realised you were right. I started looking for my birth mother.'

Holly's throat closed up, the food in her mouth suddenly seeming impossible to swallow.

'I found her, Holly. I lied to you when I said I had no interest in who she was. I applied for my natural birth certificate a few years ago when things were getting difficult in my marriage but with all the drama of the divorce I didn't feel able to cope with what I might find.'

Holly's eyes were as wide as saucers.

'After our talk, I made the effort to trace her. I found out where she is living and I wrote her a letter. When I got back from Hong Kong there was a letter waiting for me. It was from her. She wants to meet up with me, Holly. We're going to be reunited and it's all thanks to you,' he said, placing his hand over hers on the table.

Finally, Holly was able to swallow her food.

'She's alive?' Holly asked, unable to keep the surprise from her voice.

'Very much so.'

'Oh Nick. I'm so happy for you,' Holly said, recovering from the shock. 'Really, really happy.' Her heart was singing but her brain was working overtime. If this Nick was not her twin brother she would start to look for him as soon as she got back to England.

'She sounds really nice, Holly. Her circumstances were not dissimilar to yours with Harry, except she was younger than you were and her boyfriend walked out on her when she refused to have an abortion. But for her sticking to her guns, I would never have existed. She said it broke her heart giving me up for adoption but she simply couldn't cope with both babies on her own. She obviously wasn't as strong and determined as you were, Holly.'

'Things were different around the time we were born. There wasn't so much help available for single mothers. I don't think I would have been able to manage it then either and certainly not with twins. Does she still live in Nottingham?'

'No. She got herself a job as a chambermaid in a hotel in Jersey, fell in love with a local boy and they got married. She's lived there ever since. As well as my sister, they've got two grown-up sons, who are married with kids of their own. I've got this whole extra family that I may never have known anything about if it hadn't been for you.'

Nick's eyes were sparkling in the dim light. Holly had a sudden urge to hug him but stopped herself. If he had been her twin it would have been a brotherly hug but now she knew for sure they were unrelated, she didn't want to appear too forward. He had been tucking into his food throughout his revelation; Holly, however, had barely touched hers. Her emotions were running riot. Not only was she delighted that Nick had tracked his mother down and they were going to meet, it also opened up possibilities for them to get to know each other better.

'So, come on then, what was it you wanted to tell me?' he asked.

'It's not important now,' she answered.

'You're not cross with me for sharing my news first are you?'

'Don't be ridiculous. Of course not.'

'Then tell me,' Nick said.

Holly took a deep breath. 'Well firstly, you're right. I have been avoiding speaking to you.'

'I knew it,' Nick said. 'I'd started to think I was imagining it but I knew it deep inside. Why?'

'I'd made a discovery when I was sorting through my parents' things. I found a birth certificate belonging to a baby boy born to my parents on the day I was born. The name of the baby was Nicholas.' Holly examined Nick's face for a reaction but there was none, he was simply waiting for her to continue. 'When I took Harry to the hospital to see my mum just before she died, she got confused. She asked me if I'd brought the boy and I said yes, and introduced her to Harry. She said that wasn't his name. The boy she was referring to was called Nicholas or Richard but he had been taken away from her. Helen had told me that the dementia often made Mum confused so I didn't question her about it, and then she died. It wasn't until I found the birth certificate that it dawned on me: there must have been twins. The name, the date of birth, the city.... I put two and two together...' Holly's voice trailed off.

'And came up with five,' Nick said, finishing her sentence for her.

Holly nodded.

'You thought I was the Nick whose birth certificate you had found? You thought I was your long-lost twin brother?'

Holly nodded again.

'Then why on earth didn't you share your suspicions with me? Why did you just go silent on me?'

'You had told me you weren't interested in finding your real mother. I thought I had inadvertently found her for you, plus a sister and a half-sister you weren't expecting. I didn't know what to do.'

'So what changed? Why were you suddenly so desperate to tell me tonight?'

'Two reasons. When the waitress mentioned twin babies, I presumed she had seen that you and I were related.' Holly shook her head. 'I know. Stupid, aren't I? As if a complete stranger would know that just by holding my hand.'

'What was the other reason?'

A slow flush started to creep up Holly's neck. 'When you said you had something to tell me, I thought…' she cleared her throat, 'I thought, maybe you were going to tell me that you had feelings for me which would have been awful in view of me believing that we were twins.'

It was Nick's turn to nod. 'Yes, I can see that,' he said, his face giving nothing away. 'But if I were to tell you that now, what would you say?'

Holly's heart started thumping in her chest. She looked into Nick's green eyes that so closely resembled her own. 'I would have to confess to having feelings for you too.'

'Good. Then you won't mind too much if I do this.' Nick leaned towards her and ever so gently brushed her lips with his. 'I've been wanting to do that for the longest time,' he said.

A thousand explosions went off in Holly's heart. If the slightest brush of his lips could provoke that kind of reaction what would it be like when they were able to enjoy a proper kiss?

Ling reappeared with their main course, temporarily preventing any further contact between them. She smiled knowingly as she placed the earth-baked fish on the table in front of them, along with a dish of noodles and pak choy. She was about to leave them in peace when Holly stopped her.

'Ling, you were remarkably accurate with your initial assessment of me but what did you mean when you mentioned twin babies? You're right, Nick has twins but they are both boys and they're grown up now.'

'I did not know that,' she said, 'because I have not held his hand. What I saw is that you two will be blessed with twins.'

CHAPTER 49

Holly reluctantly waved goodbye to Nick from the entrance of her hotel. The whole evening had been extraordinary from the moment she had discovered that Nick was not related to her.

They had eaten the divine food Ling had placed in front of them and talked non-stop about each other's lives, both anxious to make up for lost time. After dinner, they walked hand in hand along Hong Kong's vibrant streets, drinking in the colour and diversity of their surroundings, with huge smiles on their faces. As midnight approached, Nick flagged down a taxi.

'We need to get you back to Repulse Bay,' he said, 'and then I'll head back to Kowloon.'

'There's no need for you to come all the way back to my hotel with me,' Holly said, hoping that Nick would disagree.

'You're right; I don't need to. But I want to,' he said with finality, climbing into the back of the taxi alongside her.

She rested her head on his shoulder, totally at ease, and they talked some more, only periodically interrupting the flow of conversation with a kiss.

Neither had suggested they should spend the night together, despite Holly feeling sure it was something they both wanted to happen. The heels of her shoes click-clacked, echoing across the marble floor of the hotel reception, empty apart from the night porter.

Holly already had her itinerary for the next day planned out with a trip across the Chinese border to gather information for her Liberty Sands blog. She knew, however fabulous the experience was, that she would be counting down the hours until she could meet up with Nick to spend the evening together. He had suggested she should arrive at his hotel around five and told her to bring her bathing costume so that they could have a refreshing swim after the heat and humidity of the day.

He had also made mention of the huge Jacuzzi on one of the hotel's terraces. 'When you're sitting in it,' he had said, 'it's almost as though you are sitting in the harbour itself. Not that you'd want to, of course, cleaned up or not.'

Holly could feel herself blushing at the thought of revealing her body to Nick, clad only in a bikini. I hope he likes curves, she thought, as the lift arrived at her floor and she stepped out into the corridor. At least it will lessen the shock when he sees me totally naked, she mused, sliding the key card into the slot on her door. It was an eventuality Holly was certain would occur, it was simply a matter of when. Being alone with Nick, without the complication of her on/off relationship with Philippe, had made her feel complete for the first time in her life. She had thought she had found true love with Philippe, but now realised it was something that needed to happen to set her free from her infatuation with Gareth. He had been the catalyst to allow her to move on with her life: the one before 'the one'. She knew now what it must have felt like when Rosemary and Robert met. Rosemary had told her that within hours she knew Robert was the man she wanted to spend the rest of her life with. They were soulmates, meant to be together, and Holly believed she had finally found hers, in Nick.

The light was blinking on the phone by her bedside, indicating that there was a message for her. It's probably the tour guide reminding me of the horribly early 7 a.m. pick-up, she thought, lifting the telephone receiver. It wasn't. It was a message from Harry.

'Hi, Mum, I tried you on your mobile but you didn't answer.'

Holly's ecstatic mood evaporated in an instant and her heart was gripped with fear. Oh my God, something's happened to Rosie, she thought, realising she had turned her phone off in the restaurant and hadn't turned it back on.

Harry's voice continued. 'Don't panic, which I know you'll be doing because you're you. Rosie's fine.'

Holly expelled the breath she had been holding.

'Just give me a call as soon as you get this message. It's important. Love you.'

Holly scrabbled in the bottom of her bag for her phone and waited impatiently as it kicked into life, the screen taking an eternity to illuminate. She keyed in her passcode, pacing back and forth and, as soon as she had a signal, punched in Harry's number, giving no thought to the time of day in the UK. He picked up on the third ring.

'Hi, Mum. I hope you're not panicking?'

'What's wrong, Harry?' she asked impatiently. 'You

never ring me while I'm away.'

'Calm down, Mum. I've found something out that I thought you should know about as soon as possible.'

'What is it?'

'Geoff found an envelope in the back of one of the books you gave him. He thought it might be personal to your family so he sent it home with Amy.' He paused, 'I opened it, Mum.'

'Well, what is it?'

'It's a death certificate.'

Holly's grip tightened on the receiver.

'It's dated the twenty-first of July 1974 and the name on it is Nicholas Wilson. It seems you were wrong about Nick being your twin brother.'

Holly tried to process the information.

'Are you okay, Mum?'

'Yes,' Holly replied, sinking on to the bed. 'I already knew Nick wasn't my brother. He told me over dinner tonight that he'd traced his real mother. How did Nicholas die?'

'It says "sudden infant death syndrome". Isn't that cot death? I'm so sorry, Mum.'

Holly was too choked up to speak. It was the one thing she had been terrified of when Harry was a baby. She had followed all the instructions about sleeping him on his back, with his feet against the foot of his crib and his head uncovered, and, if he was particularly quiet, she would get a mirror and hold it by his nose to make sure he was breathing. Poor Nicholas, she thought, being denied a chance to live. Why him and not me? A tear rolled from the corner of Holly's eye, then another and another.

'Are you crying?'

'Yes,' Holly sniffed, 'and I don't even really know why. Is it for the death of a twin brother I never knew I had and whose death will never be explained to me because the only two people who were there are both now dead? Or is it because I feel guilty for being relieved that Nick isn't related to me?'

'Maybe it's a bit of both, Mum, and that's okay.'

'Harry?'

'Yes, Mum?'

'I think I'm in love with Nick.'

'I know, Mum, otherwise why would you have been so upset when you thought he was your brother? Just like me and Amy, you two seem to be the perfect fit.'

Holly allowed herself a watery smile.

'We're not going to rush into things too quickly but I don't want to waste precious time either, particularly after what happened to Robert and Rosemary. You never know what life has got in store for you.'

'Don't overthink it, Mum, just follow your heart. I should let you go, this call will be costing you a fortune, but I wanted you to know about your baby brother dying so that you could stop avoiding Nick.'

'Do you think we would be able to find out where Nicholas was laid to rest?'

'Probably. Why?'

'I think I'd like to visit his grave.'

'If that's what you want to do, we'll find him. Although it happened nearly forty years ago, it's never too late to say goodbye.'

CHAPTER 50

One Year Later

Robert took a sip of his red wine, savouring the taste in his mouth for a moment before swallowing and feeling the warmth it brought to his chest. The sun would soon begin its descent towards the horizon with the promise of a glorious sunset, transforming the virtually cloudless sky from brilliant blue to shades of orange and pink. It was a perfect end to another perfect day in Mauritius, his only sadness being that his wife Rosemary wasn't there to share it with him.

He fervently hoped she would have approved of the changes he had made to Sunset Cottage, doubling it in size while maintaining the colonial style and keeping many of the original features. He needed the three additional bedrooms for when he had guests to stay, now that he had his adopted extended family, but he had also wanted to change it sufficiently to prevent Holly from feeling awkward in the space she had once shared with Philippe.

Although Philippe had distanced himself from Holly, particularly after hearing of her wedding plans, he had kept in regular contact with Robert for news and photographs of his baby daughter. He had visited England only twice in the last year and on both occasions had spent Friday morning with Rosie while Holly was at the television studios, returning her safely to Valley View before Holly returned from work. Nick had thoughtfully absented himself.

'You can't avoid Holly for ever,' Robert had said.

'I know, and I don't want to, but it's all too fresh at the moment,' Philippe had replied. 'Maybe one day we'll all be able to go out for a pizza together but I'm not ready for that yet.'

So as not to confuse the little girl, Rosie called Philippe 'Papa' and Nick, 'Dada.' It was Philippe's suggestion.

Down on the sand, below the house, Robert could see Rosie playing with her big brother, the two blond heads close together, concentrating on building a fort out of coral. She really is the most adorable little girl, he thought. My only real regret in selling up and moving out here is that I see so much less of her than I would like to.

Nick and Holly had matched the original offer Robert had received and rejected on his house in Surrey. Because it was them he had accepted, feeling as though he was keeping the house in the family. There was however one proviso: they would have to retain the live-in housekeeper/gardener, which they were more than happy to do. Robert had offered Helen a job before she had chance to consider any nursing roles and she had accepted without hesitation. Her passion was gardening and she could barely believe she was going to be paid to indulge it while living in a stunningly beautiful house. Her new post would also include being nanny to baby Rosie.

Further along the beach, Amy's distinctive strawberry-blond hair caught the breeze as she walked along the shoreline, occasionally stopping and bending down. Robert smiled. Clearly she had been sent on a coral-gathering expedition while the craftsmen did the building. They were both so good with Rosie. Robert prayed they would be blessed with the gift of children that had been denied to him and Rosemary.

A movement closer to the house caught his attention. Under the shade of a badamier tree, Holly was stirring. She obviously needed that nap, Robert thought, after the excitement of the wedding the previous day.

Everything had gone exactly as planned. The Plantation House Hotel had set up an altar under a beautiful arch bedecked with real flowers, and laid out seating for the guests on the beach in front of Roberto's restaurant, where the reception party was being held. At 5 p.m., when the heat of the day had subsided, the happy couple had taken their place in front of assembled friends and family and vowed to love each other until death do they part. The kiss was lingering but no one minded and there was a moment of humour when the best man, Hugo, caught the bouquet the bride had thrown over her shoulder.

The party had continued long after the newlyweds made their excuses to leave and Robert reckoned there would be a few sore heads currently en route to the airport for their flights home. He was pleased that Megan and Gareth had been able to make the journey. Despite the obvious challenges of walking and using his wheelchair on soft sandy pathways it was a day that would live in his memory for ever.

From his vantage point, he could see Holly was chatting with Harry but from that distance her words were lost against the rumble of the waves on the reef. He was about to call out to them both but stopped as Nick approached from behind Holly's sunbed, laid his hands on her shoulders and kissed the top of her head. Robert's heart lurched. He was truly happy for Nick and Holly but seeing them together underlined just how much he had lost when Rosemary passed away.

Holly turned her head to look up at her husband and in doing so must have spotted Robert on the veranda.

'Come down and join us,' she shouted, moving her arm in a beckoning gesture in case he was struggling to hear.

Robert shook his head and indicated his glass of wine. 'I might trip on the steps,' he called back.

'It's only six o' clock. How many glasses have you had?'

Robert turned. 'You're not nagging me are you, Helen?' he said, a smile playing at the corner of his mouth. 'It's actually my first of the evening; I didn't want to intrude on their family time.'

'I know what you mean. They all look so happy. I thought I'd stay out of the way too and help Delphine in the kitchen. She was just asking what time we would like dinner.'

'In about an hour, I would think. We don't want to be too late for Rosie, and Holly must be pretty shattered after yesterday. She's only got another eight weeks to go and it must be extra tiring carrying twins.'

'It's amazing how she is still managing to do everything and the timing couldn't be better in terms of *On The Sofa* and their summer break.'

'What a year it's been.'

'An incredible year, I'd say, Robert.'

'Bobbit!'

Robert spun round to see Rosie and Harry standing at the top of the steps leading from the beach.

'What did she say?'

Harry laughed. 'I think that must be her first attempt at saying Robert.'

'Bobbit, Bobbit, Bobbit,' Rosie chirruped, running towards Robert as fast as her sturdy little legs could carry her and launching herself at him moments after he had put his wine glass down. He swung the delighted toddler high into the air.

'Clever girl,' he said, kissing her on the end of her nose. 'That's made my day.'

'Mum sent us up here to fetch you two down to the beach. She said she won't take no for an answer and to bring Delphine too because she needs her photography skills again. She reckons it's going to be a perfect sunset and wants to use it as a backdrop for another family photo.'

Robert felt a warmth inside that had nothing to do with the red wine.

'You go ahead, Helen,' he said, handing Rosie back to Harry, 'and I'll get Delphine.'

He went inside, but before going to the kitchen to fetch his housekeeper, he crossed to his desk and picked up his wallet. He removed the photograph of his late wife and the tiny white feather nestled next to it and slipped them into the pocket of his linen shirt.

'It wouldn't be the whole family without you, my darling,' he murmured. 'Delphine,' he called out, 'your services are required on the beach.'

Minutes later, the pair of them were making their way down the weathered wooden steps and on to the white sugary sand, Delphine wiping her floury hands on her apron as she went.

'Hurry up, you two,' Holly urged, focusing her attention on the line-up in front of her. 'We've only got a couple of minutes before the sun starts disappearing over the horizon.'

'Where do you want me?' Robert asked.

'In between Helen and Harry and I'll slot in between Amy and Nick on the other side,' she said, handing the camera to Delphine. 'Harry, you and Amy hold hands, with your bodies facing the sunset but turn your faces back towards the camera, leaving just enough of a gap to see the path of the sun glittering across the sea towards you. Are you ready, Rosie?'

Her daughter nodded, a look of concentration on her face. She was sitting on the sand, in the centre of the group, holding an intricately carved dodo with a baby dodo inside, suspended from ribbons in the colours of the Mauritian flag.

'Good girl. Remember to look at the camera, won't you. How is it looking, Delphine?'

'Very good. Smile everyone,' Delphine said, depressing the button on the camera.

'Let me have a quick look,' Holly said, moving as swiftly as the soft sand would allow. 'We still have a few more moments before we start to lose the sun to take another shot if anyone was blinking.'

She reached for the camera from Delphine, the diamonds from her rings glinting in the dying rays of the sun, and cupped her hands around it to create enough shade to view the image on the screen. It was a perfect picture of the people she loved most in the world and it brought a lump to her throat. As intended, it was a re-creation of the photograph Delphine had taken in the same spot seven months earlier, the only difference being in that picture, she and Nick had been the bride and groom.

ACKNOWLEDGEMENTS

Thanks so much to everyone who has read the Liberty Sands trilogy and provided me with such positive feedback. I'm thrilled that you all cared as much about my characters as I did when I was writing about them, and I must admit to feeling bereft now that their story is told. I hope you all approve of my choice for Holly.

To Justine Taylor, my copy editor, thank you for your wonderful email after receiving the first draft of *It's Never Too Late To Say…* She said, 'It's been really lovely to see how your writing has progressed over these three books.' Trust me, Justine; I couldn't have done it without your knowledge and guidance. Once again I gave you a very tight deadline and you delivered. I will try and allow more time for the next one! And yes, there will definitely be more books.

Another member of the team is Yvonne Betancourt, my formatter. Once again a great job from you and I think the corrections list was a little shorter this time round?

The covers of *Life's a Beach and Then…* and *If He Really Loved Me…* have both received lots of compliments but one of my friends at QVC, Nat Gray, who has an eye for these sorts of things, thinks this cover is the best of the trilogy. I couldn't possibly comment as, like children, we shouldn't have favourites! It has been fun working with Angela Oltmann on this one, particularly getting the position of the 'giant' baby right!

To everyone at Ripped thank you for your support, belief and tweeting.

My family are the most important people in my life and each of you have helped me in your own way to write the Liberty Sands trilogy, from inspiration for characters to encouragement when I wondered if I had bitten off more than I could chew. Thank you from the bottom of my heart – I hope you know how much I love you.

OTHER BOOKS BY THIS AUTHOR

Life's a Beach and Then…
The Liberty Sands Trilogy Book 1

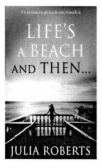

Holly Wilson has landed a dream job but there is one provision… she must keep it secret, and that means telling lies. Holly hates telling lies. Her latest assignment has brought her to the paradise island of Mauritius where she meets a British couple, Robert and Rosemary, who share a tragic secret of their own. The moment they introduce Holly to handsome writer, Philippe, she begins to fall in love, something she hasn't allowed herself to do for twenty years. But Philippe has not been completely honest and when Holly stumbles across the truth, she feels totally betrayed.

If He Really Loved Me…
The Liberty Sands Trilogy Book 2

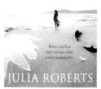

History is about to repeat itself in Holly Wilson's life… or is it? Single mum, Holly and her son Harry have an enviable relationship but when Harry discovers she is pregnant again and, for reasons unknown to all but herself, intends to raise the baby alone, he begins to question her decision not to tell him about his own father, who abandoned them before his birth. Upon discovering his father's name, Harry secretly embarks on his search for the truth and uncovers a tragic story. Still reeling from what he has learned, an extraordinary twist of fate brings Harry and Philippe, the father of Holly's unborn child, face to face. Should Harry tell him?

Available on **amazon.co.uk**

One Hundred Lengths of the Pool
Preface *publishing*

One Hundred Lengths of the Pool is a memoir exploring Julia's extraordinary life, including surviving the killer disease polio and against all odds becoming a professional dancer. That was the start of a long and varied career in the entertainment industry. In a unique book, each of the hundred lengths is associated with a special moment or memory from her life. However, there is an extra length of the pool that she didn't expect to swim and it has changed her life completely, testing her belief in her favourite saying, 'That which does not kill us, makes us stronger...'

Available on **amazon.co.uk**

CPSIA information can be obtained at www.ICGtesting.com
Printed in the USA
BVOW05s2138240516

449375BV00003B/23/P